THE BELLWETHER EFFECT

I have been a Lance Secretan fan and follower since we first met in 2010. Since then, I have read his books, learned from him, teamed up with him, and I have enjoyed so much the way he inspires others around him. *The Bellwether Effect* is not just a great book for leaders who seek to inspire and become better partners with their colleagues, but it has also helped me to think about myself and the change I want to help achieve in Microsoft and the world.

—CESAR CERNUDA, PRESIDENT, MICROSOFT, LATIN AMERICA

The Bellwether Effect not only provides terrific practical advice for leaders in rethinking routine, it also challenges leaders to be courageous in evolving the way they lead and manage teams. Like all previous generations of workers, today's workforce is looking for leaders who inspire and teach, and for organizations that serve a bigger purpose beyond shareholder returns. This book is an insightful read that shows how each of us can be a force for change in work and life.

—BRUCE D. BROUSSARD, PRESIDENT & CEO, HUMANA INC.

I was introduced to Lance Secretan and his work by a colleague in 2015. Since then, he has become a dear friend, advisor, mentor, and coach. *The Bellwether Effect* delivers a deeply insightful message that reveals an understanding of the human passion and offers a fresh approach to leadership. Thank you, Lance, for your wisdom, which will enable leaders to bring about positive change within our corporations, communities, and the world.

—JAMES D. WILSON, CHAIRMAN & CEO,
WILSON TRANSPORTATION & LEASING GROUP CANADA

This is one of those rare books that look you in the eye and touch your heart and mind. It is brilliantly simple, very pragmatic, absolutely real, and profound at the same time. This book will be a wonderful, conscientious companion to many, including me!

—RAJA RAJAMANNAR, CHIEF MARKETING AND
COMMUNICATIONS OFFICER, MASTERCARD

Unemployment is at an all-time low. The stock market is at a historic high, with corporate profitability soaring. Yet employee satisfaction remains at remarkable lows. In healthcare, over 55 percent of our physicians and over 35 percent of our nurses are showing signs of burnout. More profit, less life satisfaction. What's the answer to this modern-day dilemma? Dr. Secretan reminds us that leadership is the key. Without the Higher Ground Leadership® model he outlines in *The Bellwether Effect*—a return to the core attributes of great leadership—we are destined to repeat the folly of past generations and put patient safety, quality, as well as financial stability in the entire field of healthcare at risk. A straightforward message of love and caring in leadership is much needed in this time of instability—thank you, Lance!

— JACK COX, MD MMM, SVP, CHIEF QUALITY OFFICER,
PROVIDENCE ST. JOSEPH HEALTH

The insights Lance brings to corporate culture and management are always unique, refreshing, and frequently uncomfortable for leaders to hear. This book is no exception. The list of eight ineffective things companies do could certainly be expanded, but these are right on point. Plenty of "ineffective" around. Makes you think.

—MICHAEL B. MCCALLISTER,
RETIRED CHAIRMAN AND CEO, HUMANA INC.

As a CEO of a large health system, our organization engaged Lance and his team at the Secretan Center to guide a cultural change that strengthened the leadership skills throughout our organization and thus enhanced our success. *The Bellwether Effect* is the most complete description of strategies we used to improve our performance, and it is simply the best description of mistakes organizations make and suggestions for positive change that I have read. This book is refreshingly practical and has many how-to examples that can be used by leaders who wish to find a new way to create positive change. Every leader can profit from Secretan's thinking on leadership and change. *The Bellwether Effect* ought to be considered an owner's manual for all leaders wishing to understand why methods often used are not working and how we can inspire a new model of leadership. This book is just what most leaders need.

—JOSEPH C. CALVARUSO, SENIOR VICE PRESIDENT, OHIO HEALTH

The Bellwether Effect opens your mind to things and places to which you may resist going. It forces you to look inside yourself at things that you rationally understand but have difficulty getting your mind around emotionally. Lance's arguments force you into an intellectual corner, requiring you to respond in some fashion. In short, Lance takes away the normal hiding places and the easy bailouts. Looking at the paradigm shifts for leadership that Lance describes and his take on love in the workplace, for example, will require commitment and courage from the average reader. This is a rare opportunity to impact the future direction of the world.

—DAVE BLAIR, FOUNDER, BRANTAS PERFORMANCE INC.

Leaders today require new skills that are born from an inner wisdom that is informed by the emerging business models of the 21st century. In *The Bellwether Effect*, Dr. Lance Secretan shares deep insights into the critical leadership attributes that are essential to nourishing a successful organization—an organization that balances the needs of *all* stakeholders, including employees, shareholders, the community, and the planet. Lance shares his considerable experience in this fresh, informative new book. I highly recommend it. It's a book I covet for being both an interesting read and the North Star for leadership in our world today.

—STEVE FARRELL, WORLDWIDE EXECUTIVE DIRECTOR, HUMANITY'S TEAM

This may be one of the most consoling pieces of writing ever published on the subject of leadership. Secretan lays bare why the fear-based, dangling-carrot style that's been practiced since the dawn of the industrial revolution is failing us miserably, and what's to be done about it. He explores a holistic, values-centered approach based on love that inspires prosperous outcomes—for the individual, the organization, and the planet.

—GINA MAZZA, AUTHOR OF *Everything Matters, Nothing Matters*
(St. Lynn's Press), www.ginamazza.com

The Bellwether Effect is the "how-to" guide from Lance's previous book *The Spark, the Flame, and the Torch*. Lance, thanks for helping me to dig deep and discover a new and inspiring way to lead.

—ALLAN THOMPSON, MAYOR, TOWN OF CALEDON, ONTARIO

Municipal governments around the world have a direct influence on improving the quality of life of residents. In order to implement positive change, a municipality needs to have an inspiring workplace that embraces a sense of unity of purpose, which translates into progressive, open, and inclusive policies both internally and externally, resulting in the building of a great city. This is not simple or easy, and *The Bellwether Effect* can clearly point municipal governments in the right direction.

—Rick Goldring, Mayor, City of Burlington, Ontario

Twenty-five years ago, I was appointed CEO of a bankrupt company that was actively engaged in most of the eight destructive practices described in this book as well as some others, with the added excitement of two major shareholders at war. Lance and his message then were the catalysts for change that transformed this company into a profitable market leader in which the people truly were the company's most valuable asset. I have applied the learnings from those first encounters with Lance throughout my career. Lance's message remains as important today as it was then, and *The Bellwether Effect* is a timely reminder for some of us and an important new lesson for new leaders. The unrelenting growth and importance of data, technology, and algorithms, combined with the increased pressure to produce results more quickly, have blurred the view of the continuing crucial relevance of human beings within companies and their relationships with each other, as well as their relationships with other constituents, customers, vendors, bankers, and shareholders.

In *The Bellwether Effect*, Lance once again challenges all of us to re-examine the environment we create in our companies and to cultivate, cherish, and inspire the human factor. Difficult times can cause companies and leaders to regress to more authoritarian command-and-control practices. Lance's message in this book—of respect and love for the individual and the importance of inspiration in leadership—is a reminder that the people in companies are the most important factor through good times and bad.

—Robert H. R. Dryburgh, CEO and Corporate Director

In *The Bellwether Effect*, Lance shows a compelling, inspiring, and visionary path for today's organizations to move forward and re-invent corporate life and leadership. Many of his suggestions can be put into place with immediate impact, not only doing the right things, but also doing them right. Start your journey as a better (inspiring) leader today. This book will help you create and sustain effective transformational change in your organization.

—SYLVIA B. VOGT, PRESIDENT, CARNEGIE BOSCH INSTITUTE FOR INTERNATIONAL MANAGEMENT AT CARNEGIE MELLON UNIVERSITY

The Bellwether Effect is a thought-provoking read for current and aspiring leaders. Lance Secretan makes the case for leadership that inspires and embraces the progressive outcomes of an innovative Values-centered Leadership® model. Straightforward leadership practices that will redefine an organization's culture and outcomes.

—BILL JENSEN, CEO, TELLURIDE SKI & GOLF, LLC

The Bellwether Effect makes the most compelling case for change (half of us are unhappy with our jobs; three-quarters would quit if they could) while offering a deeply researched analysis of how we arrived at this alarming state. Then, and this is of even greater value, Secretan outlines the steps that will get us back on an inspiring course. Doing so unlocks the high potential that is inside each of us, and when potential is unlocked, we live better, we work better, and we love better. This is not a guidebook for the faint of heart, but the payoff is rich alignment (or harmony), the joy of authenticity, and the positive flow that comes with a sustained personal and professional balance. Read this book to quickly reach your greatest, most sustainable potential as a leader.

—KENNETH BLOOM, SENIOR CLIENT PARTNER, KORN FERRY INTERNATIONAL

Lance Secretan once again offers us a better way than our "best practices" could ever produce. If you're willing to walk a few challenging steps along a path less traveled, this book can shepherd you back to being who you really are, doing what you really love, with people you really care about—all from where you are right now. Go this better way with Lance, and you will inspire others with true effectiveness and true love.

—JOE REAGAN, FORMER CEO, LOUISVILLE AND ST. LOUIS CHAMBERS OF COMMERCE

OTHER BOOKS by LANCE SECRETAN

A Love Story:
An Intensely Personal Memoir

The Spark, the Flame, and the Torch:
Inspire Self. Inspire Others. Inspire the World.

ONE:
The Art and Practice of Conscious Leadership

Inspire!
What Great Leaders Do

Spirit@Work:
Bringing Spirit and Values to Work

Inspirational Leadership:
Destiny, Calling and Cause

Reclaiming Higher Ground:
Creating Organizations That Inspire the Soul

Living the Moment:
A Sacred Journey

The Way of the Tiger:
Gentle Wisdom for Turbulent Times

The Masterclass:
Modern Fables for Working and Living

Managerial Moxie:
The 8 Proven Steps to Empowering Employees
and Supercharging Your Company

The Bellwether Effect

Stop Following. Start Inspiring!

Lance H. K. Secretan

The Secretan Center Inc.

Copyright © 2018 The Secretan Center Inc.

Published by The Secretan Center Inc.
Caledon, Ontario, Canada

Library and Archives Canada Cataloguing in Publication Data

Secretan, Lance H. K., author   The bellwether effect : stop following, start inspiring! / Lance Secretan.

Includes index. ISBN 978-0-9865654-7-2 (hardcover)

        1. Leadership. 2. Industrial management.
3. Organizational effectiveness. I. Title.

HD57.7.S42 2018   658.4'092   C2018-901407-5

Edited by: Simone Gabbay, www.simonegabbay.com

Cover design: Eva Henry Art, www.evahenryart.com

Text design: www.WeMakeBooks.ca

Printed in Canada by Friesens Corporation

Dedicated to friends, clients, and all those upon whose shoulders I now stand

Believe nothing, no matter where you read it,
or who said it, no matter if I have said it,
unless it agrees with your own reason
and your own common sense.

THE BUDDHA

Bellwether: *noun;*

a wether, or other male sheep, that leads the
flock, usually bearing a bell; a person or thing
that assumes the leadership or forefront, as of
a profession or industry; a person or thing that
shows the existence or direction of a trend

CONTENTS

FOREWORD

It was fortuitous that I attended the Nebraska Hospital Association Annual Convention in Lincoln, Nebraska. I was also scheduled to attend the Missouri Hospital Association Annual Convention just a couple of weeks later. Given the usual busyness of the fall season and several other commitments during this same period, I reflected on the wisdom of being out of the office for both of these conventions. Even though I was looking forward to attending both, I was particularly drawn to the Nebraska Convention. As it turned out, my intuition was perfectly accurate.

As one of nearly a thousand audience members for the first keynote address of the convention, presented by Lance Secretan, I found myself "hanging on" to every word he said—I had never before seen an audience so captivated. Secretan's focus was on the differences between motivation and inspiration.

The speaker's work and message confirmed my own accumulated beliefs and convictions—and I asked myself, "Why have I not been more assertive and deliberate in teaching and modeling these leadership behaviors in a more loving and inspiring manner?" Why had I missed so many opportunities during my career to make personal

and professional lives more enjoyable for so many—
and encourage them to dream more, personally and on
behalf of the organizations I had been called to serve?

A short time later, I participated in the Higher
Ground Leadership® Retreat at the Secretan Center in
Ontario, Canada, personally hosted by Secretan, and
soon after, two other members of our leadership team
signed up for the retreat as well. A few months later, all
seven of our leadership team members had shared this
same experience, under Dr. Secretan's personal tutelage.

As a result, we are transforming our organization
through the application of Higher Ground Leadership®
and implementing the innovative concepts put forward
in *The Bellwether Effect*. This is a remarkable piece of
literary work that advances the merits and power of
"inspiration" versus "motivation" and "dreams" versus
"mission statements." Secretan teaches that "motivation
consists of a combination of two pressure points: fear
and material rewards (or punishments). Motivation is
seldom about the other person, but more often about
me... Motivation is largely an attempt to alter or control
the behavior of others, raise performance standards,
change attitudes or beliefs or exploit capacity. When we
come from this position, we are working principally on
the *social self*, tapping into and exploiting the fears of
the person we are trying to motivate, relying on shaming,
bribing, rewarding, threatening, or pressuring—all of

which trigger the primal fear instincts." Secretan helps the reader understand how corporate America has come to develop and practice these behaviors and why we need to change from what I now see as archaic behaviors.

In contrasting motivation, Dr. Secretan reminds us that "Inspiration is intrinsic. Unlike motivation, it does not come from fear, but from love. It is not about me— it is almost exclusively about *you*. Great leaders and coaches want to inspire others to grow, to accomplish *their* objectives, to shine, to reach *their* potential and splendor. Any rewards for these inspiring coaches and leaders come from the joy they experience when helping others to reach *their* own goals or become larger as fully realized human beings. Therefore, inspiration is an act of love and service to others, whereas motivation is self-centered...inspiration is aimed at the essential self—the soul of another, and is most often generated from within—the inspirer is merely the facilitator of the inspired."

For most of my years as a hospital CEO, I have openly subscribed to and promoted *servant leadership*. As a reflection of our organization's commitment to servant leadership, we have even drawn our organizational chart upside down, with the patient on top and our leadership team at the bottom, to connote our responsibility to support and encourage all departments and staff in the delivery of high-quality patient care to those we have been called to serve.

I have also professed that even though we are in the business of providing health care, our very basic business is one of building *collaborative relationships*. I believe that it is one thing to cooperate, it is quite another to co-labor—and good things fall out of good relationships!

I am the same leader who in the past would openly and genuinely make these bold statements while also tolerating performance appraisal systems that rated and ranked individual performance through processes providing little, if any, value and that were often demoralizing, self-serving, created competitive relationships, and were rarely inspiring. Strangely, even though I tolerated such business processes, I never had a good feeling about any of them—and yet, like the "copyfrog" that Secretan writes about in the Afterword of this book, I did nothing to change them. I am reminded of a pastor friend's comment several years ago, when he said, "even a dog knows when he/she has done something wrong."

I am humbled to say that, throughout my 45+ years in progressive leadership roles, Lance Secretan's work has impacted me more, personally and professionally, than all of the many other leadership principles and programs combined. Most importantly, his work is now impacting our employees and organization through a more inspiring approach, which includes the realization of personal and organizational dreams, greater employee gratification and ownership, enhanced patient care, creativity in services and programs, reduction in turnover, and higher performance. This reaffirms a personal conviction that "it is never too late to do the right thing"—and for us, Higher Ground Leadership® is the right thing!

I take strength in knowing that inspiration is genuine, lasting, and originates deeply from within each of us and is not just a temporal, topical solution found in many of the tactical, so-called motivational maneuvers we have inflicted on staff and organizations over time. None of these were designed for distance or duration—they are generally just a "flash in the pan."

Lance Secretan has provided a license for me, and so many others, to do the right thing, regardless of what some corporate voices (or Bellwethers) may advocate. He reminds us that "the employee is now the new customer" and that "leadership is about inspiring people, and people—every one of us—are inspired by dreams." I am also struck by his statement, "Over the last 50 years in corporate life, we have expanded our capacity to quantify, measure, and analyze, but we have stifled our capacity to dream." Equally powerful is, "A mission statement may be about *you*, but a dream is about serving *others* and how you will serve them."

Of all the riveting statements in *The Bellwether Effect*, this is my favorite: "Motivation is lighting a fire *under* someone; inspiration is lighting a fire *within* someone."

This book is bound to light a fire within all who read it and apply its message to ignite positive differences in their lives and organizations—and thus in our world.

—ROGER W. STEINKRUGER, CEO,
COMMUNITY HOSPITAL–FAIRFAX, FAIRFAX, MISSOURI

PREFACE

I've been wandering around this planet for a while. After building a very successful company from scratch into a global enterprise of 72,000 full- and part-time employees, I retired. Then I wrote a book about our 14-year odyssey and taught budding entrepreneurs in an advanced university graduate program until I realized the university wasn't the real world at all. I think Dr. Henry Kissinger knew this when he said, "University politics make me long for the simplicity of the Middle East." Within the academic community, the book wasn't a roaring success (because it tilted windmills), but it became a bestseller in the business community, and thus began my consulting career. In the 35 years since, I have worked with, mentored, and coached thousands of leaders in hundreds of organizations, and I've seen some truly brilliant things. I've also seen some really ineffective things. I have been astonished to watch discouraging things happening in organizations that cause poor morale, low performance, political intrigue, toxic cultures, and ineffectiveness.

The Bellwether Effect is written for all managers and leaders, the vast majority of whom are well intentioned, who strive daily to achieve good and successful outcomes—

to create inspiring places to work and companies with whom to do business, that are respectful of people and the environment and are high-performing in all of the important metrics while making a useful and sustainable contribution to the planet. I call this Higher Ground Leadership®,[1] an overarching theory of leadership grounded in conscious behavior to which I will frequently refer in the pages that follow.

My life's work has been dedicated to bringing greater consciousness into the workplace, teaching leaders that inspiration is a higher order of thinking that will inform our leadership in the achievement of new potential. But in working closely with leaders, I have come to realize that before we can introduce and achieve Higher Ground Leadership®, or create the kinds of work environments that are deeply inspiring, we must first remove the business processes that are deeply uninspiring.

In his book *The Inner Game of Work*,[2] coach Timothy Gallwey has shown us that all individuals and organizations have the potential (p) to achieve high levels of performance (HP), but too often interference (i) in the form of obsolete business practices or emotional interference demotivates us and puts sand in our gears.

---

1 Higher Ground Leadership® defined: http://www.secretan.com/about-us/higher-ground-leadership/

2 *The Inner Game of Work: Focus, Learning, Pleasure, and Mobility in the Workplace*, Random House, 2011, ISBN-13-978-0375758171

We can write the equation like this:

High Performance = potential − interference, or

$$HP = p - i$$

Potential and interference are closely related. We just need to introduce them in the right order. First we need to remove interfering and demoralizing business processes that are a barrier to inspiration, so that we can then concentrate on building great organizations that inspire. I have observed in my travels that there are eight old-fashioned, ineffective business practices and beliefs that have become embedded in the corporate mindset and that, collectively, present a formidable barrier to creating high-performance organizations. Besides the noble art of getting things done, there is also the noble art of removing things that add no value. Often, it is necessary to remove things in order to achieve things. We need to take away some redundant and hindering business practices so that we can add more modern approaches that inspire. *Doing so could change everything.*

The most frequent response from people with whom I shared early versions of the manuscript of this book has been, "Only eight? Really? Let me give you a few more!" or words to that effect. I admit there are probably more, but I chose what I have found to be "the big eight" during my career as an advisor to corporations and their leaders. However, if I were to add a ninth counterproductive or destructive thing that companies do to the list, it would be *hubris*—the sin of overweening pride or arrogance.[3] The inflated sense that some leaders have of themselves, their certainty of being "right," and their inflated assessment of their skills, knowledge, and value can sometimes be breathtaking, and the data shows that this is a major cause of corporate failure.[4] More humility in leadership would be a blessing, as it would lead to greater openness to fresh thinking about leadership—a subject to which I will return later, and particularly in the Afterword.

In each chapter in this book, I have not only described the counterproductive business processes, but also their antidote—what we could do differently, in a more inspiring way, to achieve the good intentions and outcomes we originally had in mind.

Nearly one in two employees is unhappy with their job,[5] and the latest global Edelman Trust Barometer reveals the largest-ever drop in trust across the institutions of government, business, media, and NGOs, with CEO credibility having dropped 12 points globally to an all-time low of 37 percent.[6]

---

3 "Rooting Out Hubris, Before a Fall," Steven Berglas, *Harvard Business Review*: https://hbr.org/2014/04/rooting-out-hubris-before-a-fall

4 "The Line between Confidence and Hubris," Tim Laseter, Strategy+Business: https://www.strategy-business.com/article/The-Line-between-Confidence-and-Hubris?gko=c7827

5 "More Than Half of US Workers are Satisfied with Their Jobs," The Conference Board: https://www.conference-board.org/press/pressdetail.cfm?pressid=7184

6 2017 Edelman Trust Barometer: https://www.edelman.com/news/2017-edelman-trust-barometer-reveals-global-implosion/

We have lost our passion for corporate life. During my presentations to audiences, I often ask them this question: "What percentage of the population do you think would leave the corporate world and pursue different interests if they had a completely free hand?" As at an auction, I start at 50 percent, and the audience will typically raise the offer until we settle at an estimate of something more than 80 percent. Why is this a tragedy? Because, apart from the human anguish and suffering that such a chronic state of discontent causes, we live in a capitalist society, one of whose main engines (besides the church and government) is commerce, and if we botch this critical source of livelihood and exchange, we risk losing everything. So reclaiming our passion for corporate life, and reinfusing work with inspiration, is not an inconsequential issue.

I wrote this book to share what I've learned in order to help the reader to reverse this trend, restore sanity and effectiveness for a frazzled employee population, create inspiring organizations that lift the hearts of people, and *make a positive difference in the world.*

And that last part is the most important. As I wrote earlier, the corporation is the most powerful institution in the world—more powerful than politics, more even than the church—it has the reach, resources, intellect, finances, and scale that cannot be matched by any other institution. Apple Inc. has more cash on hand than the

GDPs of two-thirds of the world's countries.[7] Today, the
ten biggest banks control almost 50 percent of assets
under management worldwide.[8] Three months after
Luiz Inácio Lula da Silva won his landslide victory in
Brazil's presidential elections, disappointed corporations
drove the currency down by 30 percent, $6bn in hot
money left the country, and various credit agencies gave
Brazil the highest debt-risk ratings in the world. "We
are in government but not in power," said Lula's close
aide, Dominican friar Frei Betto. "Power today is global
power, the power of the big companies, the power of
financial capital."[9] Therefore, if we want to change the
world, the corporation is the most powerful vehicle on
earth through which to attain that dream.

My hope is that this book will help you to ask some
challenging questions about why your organization
does things, and why they are done in a certain way,
and whether there might be better business processes
to consider as replacements to your existing ones. If
that turns out to be the case, I believe your load will
be lightened, your life will be more inspired, and my
objective in writing this book will be accomplished.

---

7 "These 25 Companies Are More Powerful Than Many Countries," Parag Khanna and
   David Francis, *Foreign Policy*: http://foreignpolicy.com/2016/03/15/these-25-companies-
   are-more-powerful-than-many-countries-multinational-corporate-wealth-power/
8 ibid
9 "Who's in Control – Nation States or Global Corporations?," Gary Younge, *The
   Guardian*, https://www.theguardian.com/commentisfree/2014/jun/02/control-nation-
   states-corporations-autonomy-neoliberalism

The Bellwether Effect

DISSONANCE

For a long time, I have been puzzled by the process by which companies and their leaders adopt business practices. Even more puzzling is why leaders continue to utilize these practices when they are patently long past their "best before date." This leads to *dissonance*— defined by Merriam-Webster as "lack of agreement; the dissonance between the truth and what people want to believe; especially: inconsistency between the beliefs one holds or between one's actions and one's beliefs." Dissonance is evidenced among leaders who stubbornly champion business practices, even though the majority of employees loathe them and see them as pointless or worse. This dissonance is very common in my experience. I can't count the number of times in which I have heard one story from senior leaders and an entirely different one from their direct reports. That's dissonance—the difference between the truth and what leaders want to believe. So often, senior leaders champion a policy that they believe to be efficient, effective, and warmly embraced by everyone in the organization, but if you listen to those who work with those policies or practices every day, you would likely hear a very different perspective. These business practices continue to be supported, funded, and expanded, even though the majority of employees view them as useless or even counterproductive. I am reminded of Stephen Colbert's wry observation, "I'm not a fan of facts. You see, the facts can change, but my opinion will never change, no matter what the facts are."

So let's dig into some research around this phenomenon and knit some ideas together to understand how counterproductive business practices originate, how propaganda promotes their adoption, how followers blithely embrace and implement these policies, and how they become embedded, even though the evidence shows that, in large part, they don't work.

HOW "FORERUNNERS"
INFLUENCE THEIR PEERS

Morton M. Grodzins (1917-1964), the late dean at the University of Chicago, coined the term "tipping point," a phrase he adopted from physics, where it is used to describe the incremental addition of small amounts of weight to a balanced object until it eventually "tips." In the early 1960s, Grodzins used the term to describe the phenomenon of mixed race neighborhoods in the U.S., where he showed that white families would remain in the neighborhood as long as the number of black families remained comparatively fewer, but as soon as that ratio changed, even by one, white families would begin to leave. This work was built upon by, among others, Nobel prize-winner Thomas Schelling, and in the 1980s by Mark Granovetter, who sought to explain the paradox of "situations where outcomes do not seem intuitively consistent with the underlying individual preferences"—what I referred to earlier as "dissonance." He reasoned that there is a threshold at which individual behavior influences the behavior of the surrounding group. Using the example of riots in his research, he showed that riots are usually started by one person, who appears to be what he called a *forerunner* (threshold 0), and when this act is witnessed by another, that person (threshold 1), who would never normally engage in rioting, can be emboldened to throw a brick through a window. This may be followed by another (threshold 2), and then others (threshold *n*) follow suit.

The forerunner—whom Granovetter described as threshold zero—can be thought of as a bellwether. The term "bellwether" (from the Middle English "bellewether") is a thirteenth-century word that was originally used to describe a ram, wearing a bell, that was designated as the leader of a flock of sheep. A shepherd who had lost his or her flock could locate their sheep by listening for the bellwether.

Researchers at Leeds University in the UK conducted an experiment in which 200 participants walked randomly in silence around a large hall. Within this group, a small number had been given instructions that, after a while, they were to walk in a particular manner and direction. The researchers discovered that participants eventually followed these "bellwethers" because they seemed to know where they were going. Researchers concluded that a mere 5 percent of externally appearing self-assured "bellwethers" could influence the behavior of the other 95 percent.[10] Using computational and analytical methods, scientists at Rensselaer Polytechnic Institute conducted other experiments leading to the same conclusion, finding that "when 10 percent of the population holds an unshakable belief, their belief will always be adopted by the majority of the society." They

---

10 "Sheep in Human Clothing—Scientists Reveal Our Flock Mentality," University of Leeds: http://www.leeds.ac.uk/news/article/397/sheep_in_human_clothing__scientists_reveal_our_flock_mentality

concluded that "the finding has implications for the study and influence of societal interactions ranging from the spread of innovations to the movement of political ideas."[11] The tipping point for mass adoption seems to be around 5–10 percent.

I will call this the "Bellwether Effect." In a business environment, the Bellwether Effect translates as, "Copying the business practices of those who influence group behavior." It is caused by two factors—the desire to conform and the need to mimic someone perceived as admirable in the hope that, through association, similar prestige will accrue to the copycat. The result is a mimicry epidemic that sweeps across organizations. Of course, organizations that conform have nothing to offer but their conformity.

The Bellwether Effect can be seen to play out in almost any part of society. For example, for many decades, Hollywood has known about and condoned sexual harassment, which has been a well-guarded industry secret enforced by a powerful few while being loathed by thousands—another clear example of dissonance. As far back as 1945, Maureen O'Hara, the late Irish actress, called out Hollywood for inappropriate behavior:

> "I'm a helpless victim of a Hollywood whispering campaign. Because I don't let my producer and director kiss me every morning or let them paw

---

11 "Minority Rules: Scientists Discover Tipping Point for the Spread of Ideas," *RPI News*: https://news.rpi.edu/luwakkey/2902

me they have spread the word around town that I am not a woman — that I am a cold piece of marble statuary. I guess Hollywood won't consider me as anything except a cold hunk of marble until I divorce my husband, give my baby away and get my name and photograph in all the newspapers. If that's Hollywood's idea of a woman I'm ready to quit now."[12]

Brave and authentic as Maureen O'Hara was 70 years ago, her voice was insufficiently influential to become a "threshold 0" or create a Bellwether Effect. It took 70 years and one new courageous threshold 0, Ashley Judd, followed by another (threshold 1) and then others (threshold n) who courageously followed, to create a movement. Ten years before it became a global viral campaign, Tarana Burke created the "Me Too" campaign as a grass-roots movement to reach sexual assault survivors in underprivileged communities. In 2017, actress Alyssa Milano (threshold 0) asked her Twitter followers to share their stories of sexual harassment and assault using the Twitter hashtag "#metoo," thus creating a Bellwether Effect, which was accelerated by a digital tsunami (threshold n) that fueled a global campaign involving millions of men and women telling their own personal stories. Investigations, prosecutions, and ruined careers resulted in several countries. Hollywood

12 James Rhodes, Twitter: https://twitter.com/JRhodesPianist/status/926896883083239424

(and eventually other sectors of our societies) would never be the same.

As the examples above illustrate, the Bellwether Effect can be found in many different fields, and it can have either a positive influence (early successful adopters) or a negative influence (dissonance). Let's take a look at how it plays out in business.

At one time, IBM was the ultimate Bellwether Effect forerunner. The company was so successful in its heyday that practitioners in business would look to the company as an exemplar—*the* company from whom to learn and copy because everything they did seemed to work out so well. Other Bellwether Effect forerunners, in their time, have been Procter & Gamble and GE and, in more recent years, Google, Apple, Facebook, Microsoft, and others. A few other examples of Bellwether Effect forerunners are Harvard (and *Harvard Business Review*), Stanford University, Warren Buffett, Steve Jobs, Bill Gates, and McKinsey and Company.

When GE (then a highly respected Bellwether Effect forerunner) decided to introduce a policy (now abandoned) of firing the bottom 10 percent of performers in a department or division, many companies picked up on this idea and implemented it. Under Jack Welch, GE also introduced a concept of pathological competition called "stack ranking," a system in which managers were required to grade employees against one another and rank them on a scale of one to five. It was later copied by, among others, Steve Ballmer at Microsoft, where employees derided it with the moniker "rank and yank," because lower performers were strongly encouraged to leave the company—another extreme example of dissonance. It, too, was subsequently abandoned, but by the early 2000s, 60 percent of Fortune 500 companies had copied and adopted a forced ranking system, a stunning example of the brush-fire speed at which the Bellwether Effect can move.[13]

In 1990, Michael Hammer, a former professor of computer science at MIT, published an article titled "Reengineering Work: Don't Automate, Obliterate" in the *Harvard Business Review*, which gave birth to another business process that became known as "reengineering," in which Hammer implicitly accused managers of supervising work that did not add any value for customers, and he proposed that this type of work should be eliminated, not automated. Several Bellwether copycat companies hopped on the reengineering bandwagon, and grateful consulting companies embraced a new trendy business process they could sell, creating entire divisions dedicated solely to peddling this new practice to their unsuspecting clients. Until its ultimate demise, reengineering became a code word for "you will lose your job," terrorizing employees, especially if it was

---

13 "The Performance Management Revolution," Peter Tapelli and Anna Tavis, *Harvard Business Review*: https://hbr.org/2016/10/the-performance-management-revolution

partnered with Six Sigma (6σ),[14] a set of techniques and tools for process improvement first introduced by engineers Bill Smith and Mikel J. Harry during their tenure with Motorola in 1986, when that company was a Bellwether Effect forerunner. Reengineering was loved and copied by leaders and consultants and hated by almost everyone else—dissonance at its most extreme.

The litany of failed business processes, often generated by Bellwether organizations, is long: best practices, matrix management, core competencies, benchmarking, and more, some of which we will detail in the chapters that follow.

The Bellwether Effect usually starts with a powerful, influential, and admired forerunner (threshold 0), who often promotes a business practice without sufficient consideration of the effect it will have on people— inside and outside the organization. Being a Baldrige Award winner, or making the "100 Best Companies to Work for in America" list or being ISO 9001 certified can have the same effect. Sometimes the dissonance is caused by treating the adoption of a business process as a marketing or PR project—being a company known as a thought leader and cutting-edge management pioneer enhances its image and reputation, is a magnet for bright

---

14 Six Sigma, a registered trademark of Motorola, is a statistical measure in which 99.99966% of all opportunities to produce some feature of a part are statistically expected to be free of defects, or 3.4 errors per million opportunities.

new recruits, and creates a "halo effect" with customers. But if the "new idea" is not carefully thought through (sometimes, companies want to be first and famous more than right), dissonance can be created between corporate leaders on the one hand, and their followers, customers, and the public on the other. The reputation (often self-perceived and promoted) of threshold 0 Bellwether organizations carries enough influence and reach to persuade threshold 2, 3, and then more, to become copycats and follow suit. Dissonance frequently occurs as a result, but is usually ignored. This leads to an "Emperor's New Clothes" condition in which corporate processes deemed to be useless, harmful, or ineffective by their users continue to be promoted, funded, and championed by leaders oblivious to the dissonance. Leaders will tell you all is well; followers will tell you a different story. The result: disillusioned employees and multiple roadblocks on the path toward conscious leadership and the creation of inspiring organizations.

Let's look at some of them.

TWO

From Fear to Love

THE DARK TRIAD
PERSONALITY THEORY

Fear is the ruling practice in modern organizations. Employees are afraid of their managers, of losing their jobs, being lost in bureaucracy, being replaced by robots, getting poor performance ratings, being called out publicly for missing their budgets or targets. In turn, their managers are afraid of employee theft, lawyers, risk and compliance managers, regulators, unions, banks, the IRS, the media, competitors, hackers—and a list that could probably fill this entire book. Customers are afraid of organizations. In particular, they are afraid of being duped, "surge pricing," misleading labeling, small-print contracts, failure to stand behind products and services, "voicemail jail," corruption, corporate power and over-reach, bureaucracy, environmental disasters, lying, false advertising, loss leaders—and another list that would probably fill a second book!

How many different kinds of characteristics are there in those who perpetrate fear? According to Delroy L. Paulhus and Kevin M. Williams, both professors of psychology at the University of British Columbia, the answer is three—namely, the so-called "Dark Triad" of Machiavellianism, narcissism, and psychopathy.[15] In 2002, Paulhus and Williams introduced the Dark Triad, a constellation of three conceptually distinct but empirically overlapping personality variables. The three variables are described as:

Machiavellianism: a tendency to be manipulative and deceitful. It usually stems from a lack of re-spect for, or disillusionment about, others. Machi-

15 Delroy L. Paulhus and Kevin M. Williams, "The Dark Triad of Personality: Narcissism, Machiavellianism, and Psychopathy," *Journal of Research in Personality*: http://www.sciencedirect.com/science/article/pii/ S0092656602005056

avellianism is characterized by manipulation and exploitation of others, a need to control, cynical disregard for morality, and a focus on self-interest and deception.

Narcissism: an egotistical preoccupation with self. Because of their practice of, and experience with, maintaining their self-image, people who score high for narcissism will often appear charming, but their narcissism can later lead to extreme difficulty in developing close relationships. Narcissism is characterized by grandiosity, pride, egotism, and a lack of empathy.

Subclinical psychopathy: reflecting shallow emotional responses. The relative lack of emotions and inability to "feel" results in high stress tolerance, low empathy, little guilt, and leads people scoring high in psychopathy to seek extremely stimulating activities resulting in impulsivity and a disposition toward interpersonal conflict. Psychopathy is characterized by continuing antisocial behavior, selfishness, callousness, and remorselessness.

These three—Machiavellianism, narcissism, and psychopathy—often show differential correlates but share a common core of callous manipulation—a primary cause of workplace fear. There are now many studies on the Dark Triad personality and, according to Google Scholar, nearly 30,000 citations.

In a fear-based corporation, many individuals, and often the entire culture of the organization as a whole, can seem to behave as a Dark Triad personality.

Machiavellianism plays out in the form of marketing and public relations and in social media, where it is common practice to use addictive techniques to keep people hooked in a dopamine-driven feedback loop, and in the use of lawyers to manipulate and control the behavior of others, particularly customers (who are pejoratively referred to, and dismissed as, mere "consumers"). It shows up sometimes as "fake news" and manipulative viral campaigns on social media.

Narcissism puts the corporate goals ahead of the needs of people, the public good, or the environment. Typically, narcissistic organizations are driven by such metrics as market domination, growth, sales targets, or profit objectives—all indexes of internal performance, not of external quality, service delivered, or contribution to society and the world—and all ignoring the customer.

Psychopathy is evidenced through reengineering, rightsizing, RIFs,[16] and other unfeeling behavior. Scripting, a process where employees deliver scripts to customers instead of identifying customer needs and meeting them, is a good example of how we institutionalize this unfeeling behavior.[17]

---

16 "RIF" is an acronym for "Reduction in Force"

17 An example of scripting advice can be found here: https://www.entrepreneur.com/article/220279

When all these come together, they are acted out vividly by organizations where traditionally valued leadership qualities such as "focused, driven, ruthless, and successful" are practiced—and these are based on fear. As a leader, where do you stand? You can find out with the Short Dark Triad test.[18]

Fear is the common theme that underpins the behavior of Dark Triad personalities, and fear is the main driver of motivation, the ruling theory of modern leadership and human resources policy, a concept on which I will expand in the next chapter.

MOVING FROM FEAR TO LOVE

To be loved and to love others is the first human need. Our goal—in corporations as well as the rest of our lives—is to meet the *second* most important human need—to be *inspired* and to *inspire* others—and this second need is most easily achieved by meeting the first.

I recently conducted a study of business literature and management journals to discover the most often referenced "top qualities of a great leader." Here, alphabetically arranged, is a composite list of what I found. A great leader, it is said, must be:

---

18 Open Source Psychometrics Project: https://openpsychometrics.org/tests/SD3/

Accountable	Good communicator
Adaptable	Honest
Committed to goals	Intuitive
Confident	Motivator
Creative	Positive
Decisive	Results oriented
Delegator	Strategic
Diligent	Visionary
Focused	

If your leadership heroes are George S. Patton, Douglas McArthur, Mao Zedong, Che Guevara, Alexander the Great, Napoleon, Julius Caesar, John Wayne, and the Terminator, then this will line up nicely with your worldview. (One can even find a Top 10 list of characteristics of terrible leaders![19])

Next, I researched the top qualities that individuals ascribe to their partners in a great relationship/marriage. Here, alphabetically arranged, is a composite list of what I discovered:

Affectionate	Loving
Empathetic	Makes you feel special
Forgiving	Mature
Generous and	Open-minded
serving selflessly	Passionate
Good listener	Patient
Growing together	Playful, adventurous, and fun
Honest and ethical	Respectful and independent
Interesting	Trusting
Intimate	Vulnerable

---

19 "Ten Fatal Flaws That Derail Leaders," Jack Zenger and Joseph Folkman, *Harvard Business Review*: https://hbr.org/2009/06/ten-fatal-flaws-that-derail-leaders

It's striking how different these two lists are from each other. The list does have one similarity—honesty—but for the rest, they are markedly different. It's as if we were expected to behave as two different people—as a leader on the one hand, and as a spouse, parent, or friend on the other. Of course, this is an illusion—as if it were possible for us to wake up in the morning as Doctor Jekyll, then go to work as Mr. Hyde (Goodbye, Honey, I'm going to work to be accountable, decisive, focused, and visionary!), and then return as Doctor Jekyll (Hi, Honey, I'm home to be empathetic, intimate, loving, passionate, and vulnerable!). It is hard for the authentic leader to live a double life. As Mahatma Gandhi observed, "One man cannot do right in one department of life whilst he is occupied in doing wrong in any other department. Life is one indivisible whole."

INSPIRATION COMES FROM INSPIRING RELATIONSHIPS

I consider great leaders in the same way that I look at high-performance athletes—"one indivisible whole." For example, to be at the top of one's leadership game, one needs to be in peak condition. If you are suffering from lifestyle-induced physical ailments, or if your relationships with your family are fragile or broken, then it is important to embark on a regimen (and a personal culture change) that will boost personal well-being, which, in turn, enables an individual to pursue high-performance leadership. Great leadership cannot be practiced in a vacuum. As we will discuss in Chapter 4, everything is connected. Thus, leadership that inspires both the leader and the follower is a combination of excellence across 11 variables, shown below in the coaching model we use in my company. The stronger our relationship with each of the 11 variables, the more likely we are to be "complete" or a "Whole Human®," and therefore the higher our performance as a leader. There is no separateness between these 11—if you move one, you will change all the others:

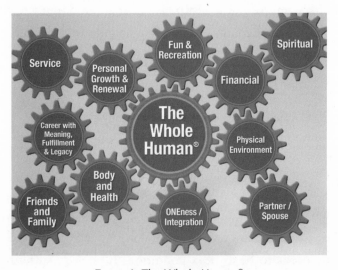

FIGURE 1: The Whole Human®

On a zero-to-ten scale, where do you stand in relation to each of these 11 variables? How strong is your relationship to all 11 variables? To be a Whole Human®, it is necessary to dial up the *relationship* to each of these in order to achieve high-performance leadership. In other words, we need to *love* each of these—our body and health, partner or spouse, family and friends, career, and so on, and ideally, they should be *congruent*. To see where you stand, complete the Congruence Wheel accessible at the link referenced in this footnote.[20]

Some would say that the primary purpose of a leader is to create shareholder wealth or increase market share and profitability. All of these are important, but the foremost purpose of a great leader is to establish great relationships (with employees, customers, shareholders, vendors, regulators, the media, the environment, etc.) because outstanding corporate performance is the natural result of outstanding relationships.

Why do we have two entirely separate sets of attributes for building relationships in different areas of our lives? If personal relationships at home are poor, it is inevitable that the strain and sadness—perhaps even anger—will be brought to work, and this will be evident to one's colleagues. If a leader cannot build successful relationships at home, why would we think they could do so at work? Several studies have shown that CEOs

---

20 The Secretan Center "Congruence Wheel": www.secretan.com/congruencewheel

with MBA degrees fare less well than those without[21]—
perhaps this is the result of learning about strategy
and spreadsheets instead of how to build inspiring
relationships. Inspiring leadership is about building
great, deep, and inspiring—and loving—relationships,
and the qualities required for doing so are universal;
they are listed in the second chart above. And if the
relationship between you and your mind, or your body,
or your spirit is broken, you might ask yourself, "How
can I strengthen my relationship with my mind, body,
and spirit—how can I fall in love with them again?"

Most of the leaders I coach are incredibly successful,
but many of them have paid a heavy price for their
success—they are out of shape, or they have poor
(sometimes non-existent) spousal, parental, or familial
relationships—and sometimes all of these. In their
own minds, they separate their failure in relationships
or health, on the one hand, from their role as a leader
on the other. This, of course, is an illusion. "Success,"
especially material success, does not necessarily equate
with being a great leader.

So leadership experts and academics are searching
for the next big thing. They're looking at teaming,

---

21 "Studies Show CEOs With MBAs More Likely to Fail," *The Globe and Mail*:
https://www.theglobeandmail.com/report-on-business/careers/management/
studies-show-ceos-with-mbas-more-likely-to-fail/article34504662/?utm_
source=Shared+Article+Sent+to+User&utm_medium=E-mail:+Newsletters+/+E-
Blasts+/+etc.&utm_campaign=Shared+Web+Article+Links and "MBA CEOs,
Short-Term Management and Performance," *Journal of Business Ethics*: https://
link.springer.com/article/10.1007/s10551-017-3450-5

collective leadership, "leadership competencies," generational difference management (*see* my blog on this[22]) and engagement, to name a few. But there is no "next big thing." There is only one thing—at home or at work—it is called *love*. It can come in many forms—the second list above covers a lot of them—and one could add many more. However, love sums up the essential quality of a great leader—love for colleagues, love for customers, love for self, love for the environment, love for the contribution they are making to a better world—in fact, love for everything good in the world in which we are blessed to live.

There is just one thing we need to teach leaders who wish to be great and to inspire others, and that is how to love, and it is surprising how many are still afraid to do so. *Love is not about maximizing what you can get; it is about maximizing what you can give.*

We all know all of this—but our antiquated mindsets tell us that love is not an appropriate concept in the workplace. Corporate life is masculine in its design, forcing many female leaders to adopt a "warrior" persona and men to constantly prove their masculinity. In her film *The Mask You Live In*, which dissects modern masculinity, American actress and documentary film-maker, Jennifer Siebel Newsom seeks to explore the effects of a culture where men are not allowed to express or even experience the full range of their emotions. She

22 The Secretan Center Inc. blog: www.secretan.com/millennial-shemennial

reminds us how this begins: "At a young age, boys learn that to express compassion or empathy is to show weakness. They hear confusing messages that force them to repress their emotions, establish hierarchies, and constantly prove their masculinity. They often feel compelled to abide by a rigid code of conduct that affects their relationships, narrows their definition of success and, in some cases, leads to acts of violence leading to what many researchers call a 'boy crisis.' Our society's failure to recognize and care for the social and emotional well-being of our boys contributes to a nation of young men who navigate adversity and conflict with an incomplete emotional skill set. Whether boys and later men have chosen to resist or conform to this masculine norm, there is loneliness, anxiety, and pain."

Are men insecure about their masculinity, especially in the corporate world? Do men believe that expressing their emotions, being vulnerable, intimate, or compassionate will make them appear weak? Do men believe that connecting emotionally with others will somehow reduce their "maleness" in the eyes of others? Of course, the opposite is true, and as the old Iroquois saying reminds us, "It takes a strong man to be gentle."

In my workshops, I ask audiences two questions: 1) "Please raise your hand if you'd like more fear and competition in your life" (not a single hand is ever raised), and 2) "Please raise your hand if you would like more love in your life" (every single person in the room always raises their hand). Of course, everybody wants more love in their lives—that's because they're human beings! And everyone to whom we report, or who reports to us, or with whom we do business or interact, is also a human being, and all of them want more love in their lives too— because they are exactly the same as we are—humans! The ancient Greeks had six definitions of love:

1. Eros – sexual passion and desire
2. Philia – deep friendship and loyalty
3. Ludus – playful love, flirting, teasing, bantering, dancing
4. Agape – love for everyone, brotherly or sisterly love (called Metta or "universal loving kindness" in the Buddhist tradition)
5. Pragma – long-standing love, often between long-married couples
6. Philautia – love of the self, what Buddhists refer to as "self-compassion"

Corporate cultures built mainly on agape—selfless love, love extended to everyone—invigorate their organizations, within as well as outside in their marketplaces, with vendors, regulators, and other "stakeholders." Philia might be described as the kind of love we hope for with our customers. In fact, Kevin Roberts, the former CEO of the advertising agency Saatchi and Saatchi, developed a bold concept to replace the dated jargon of "corporate brands." In the diagram below, it can be seen that there are two axes—the vertical one, which measures respect on a low-to-high scale, and the horizontal one, which measures love on a low-to-high scale. For a customer to "fall in love" with a product or service, it must be both highly respected and loved at the same time. Roberts describes this as "creating loyalty beyond reason," pointing out that mere *products* (commodities) appear in the bottom left corner, enjoying neither love nor respect. *Brands* appear in the top left of the quadrant, commanding respect, sometimes deeply, but not much love. Products and services appearing in the bottom right corner of the quadrant are much loved, but this love is short-lived and contains no respect. Roberts describes the products and services in the top right corner of the quadrant as "lovemarks," and organizations seek this "sweet spot" of love and respect because it is what most strongly attracts customers. Roberts has also explained that the essential ingredients of a lovemark are *mystery* (great storytelling, tapping into dreams, myths, and icons that connect emotionally and inspire, such as Harry Potter, Disney, Moleskine, John Denver, the Budweiser Clydesdales), *sensuality* (sight, smell, sound, taste, and touch, such as might be connected with brands like Cadbury, IKEA, Lego, Apple, Starbucks, Audi) and *intimacy* (commitment, empathy, and passion, for example as offered by Levis, Sharpie, Rolex, Harley-Davidson, Instagram, the Mini Cooper, and the Toyota Prius).

F<small>IGURE</small> 2: Products, Brands, Fads, and Lovemarks

Notice how the words *mystery, sensuality,* and *intimacy* draw on the list of attributes in the table above that describe the essential qualities invested by those enjoying a successful relationship or marriage. The success of an organization depends on whether its relationship with its customers is inspiring. Even more, it depends on whether its relationship with its employees is inspiring. Isn't our endgame the creation of a loving and inspiring relationship with every connection—internally and externally?

In my experience, friction in organizations arises wherever relationships are uninspiring, and where success and dreams are achieved, it is always through the seamlessness of inspiring relationships. Therefore, great organizations are those built on inspiring relationships, whereas mediocre ones rest awkwardly on the unstable quicksand of a dysfunctional culture of weak or broken relationships. There are countless examples of weak strategies that have turned into successes through inspiring partnerships or relationships and, conversely, many instances where strong strategies have failed due to ineffective and uninspiring relationships. As Mary Kay Ash observed, "A mediocre idea that generates enthusiasm will go further than a great idea that inspires no one." It isn't about the strategy; it's about the strength of the relationships—internally and externally—and how inspiring (and loving) each relationship is. Teams whose members love each other can accomplish almost anything they choose, whereas fearful teams cannot. Take the free test at the link in the footnote to determine your job burnout level and the degree to which your organization inspires your soul.[23]

Our challenge is to understand how profoundly we have misunderstood leadership and how counter-productive and dangerous this misunderstanding has become; to rethink our entire approach to teaching and practicing leadership, and to have the courage to lead in a loving and inspiring way. The fear-based, aggressive model of the warrior leader and the organization as a mechanical—not emotional—place, where you "leave

---

23 The Secretan Center Inc. Job Burnout Survey: http://www.secretan.com/tools/ assessment-tools/job-burnout-survey/

your emotions in the parking lot," is outdated. We need to see our organizations as communities and behave in ways that are consistent across all aspects of our lives—at home and at work—showing the same levels of love as we would in any other part of our lives. This will be no mean feat. But our future will depend on it. Why? Because we are exhausting people, and alienating them from work, with the old Bellwether approaches. If we replace fear with love in our workplaces, we will reach higher levels of performance than we are currently achieving with fear-based models—breakthroughs and transformations in corporate culture will be the reward. Loving—and therefore inspiring—corporate cultures will inspire communities and this, in turn, will change the world.

We are born with love, but we learn fear.

THREE

From Motivation to Inspiration

THE FAILURE OF THE "LEADERSHIP INDUSTRY"

According to the Association for Talent Development, we are spending $170 billion a year on leadership development in North America, and there are nearly 200,000 books on Amazon.com about leadership. Yet, leadership is broken everywhere. All this spending and cajoling has resulted in unhappy employees outnumbering happy ones by two to one—a disastrous return on investment. In a survey of 17,000 employees in 19 industries, the *Mind the Workplace Report*,[24] conducted by Mental Health America and the Faas Foundation, reported that 71 percent of employees were either "actively looking for new job opportunities" or had the topic on their minds "always, often or sometimes" at work. A mere 19 percent said they "rarely or never" thought about getting another job. And this dismal situation has remained unchanged for five years.[25] Mental Health America points out that this costs American business $500 billion a year! As Harvard's Barbara Kellerman has written, "The rise of leadership as an object of our collective fascination has coincided precisely with the decline of leadership in our collective estimation." Partly this is because we teach leadership like engineering—a sort of cause-and-effect, mechanical formula: If you do these three things, then these outcomes will occur. Another reason so many of these initiatives fail is that they are often presented as a completely one-sided process—to help the company achieve its objectives (narcissism). Such programs might enjoy greater "stickiness" and therefore greater effectiveness if they were also presented in a way that showed employees how the initiative would benefit them and help them to grow as complete human beings.

---

24 *Mind the Workplace Report*, Mental Health America:
   http://tinyurl.com/ybgombc7
25 "Unhappy Employees Outnumber Happy Ones By Two To One Worldwide,"
   Forbes: http://tinyurl.com/y8sa4cer

One of my clients, a global pharmaceutical company, recently shared with me a copy of their leadership development program, created in partnership with one of the world's largest consulting companies. It began with a clear statement of the program's single objective: "To align individual performance with corporate goals." In other words, the company's intention was to motivate employees so that their waking hours were dedicated to achieving the company's ambitions (share price, market share, revenue targets, etc.) while omitting any reference to how this training might benefit employee well-being or serve customers—all narcissism, and no empathy. My client wasn't encouraging me to learn from this; he was showing it to me because he was embarrassed and ashamed.

THE SOCIAL SELF AND THE ESSENTIAL SELF

We each make decisions based on one of two criteria: the ego or the soul—what I will refer to as the "social self" and the "essential self." The social self externally references, using "success" as a measure. The metric of success seeks answers to such questions as: Am I right? Will I win? Am I good enough? Will I get more (money, power, status, approval, fame)?—all being externally gauged metrics. "More" is the signature of the ego.

The social self—the persona, by which we are known to others—calibrates almost exclusively against the exterior.

The essential self internally references, using joy as a measure. The essential self is a deeper, numinous source that connects us to our higher selves. The metric of joy seeks to answer such questions as: Will this serve others? Will this make the world a better place? How can I serve? Will this bring happiness? Does this nourish my soul?—all being internally gauged metrics.[26] The essential self represents our true essence, our internal compass, what we long for and what, if supported generously by the social self, would guide us joyfully and flawlessly through our lives—as leaders and as people. But the social self constantly manipulates and overrides our thinking in order to make us conform to an external compass—what people will think and whether they will love or approve of us, our image, our shortcomings, how we will be assessed or judged, what is politically correct, whether we will succeed or fail or be triumphant, or whether our actions will enhance our careers—in other words, our level of "success"— as judged by external measures. Eckhart Tolle writes, "Why does the ego play roles? Because of the one unexamined assumption, one fundamental error, one unconscious thought. That thought is: I am not enough.

---

26 Take the Secretan Center Inc. Soulscreen Survey to determine whether your work is nourishing your soul: http://www.secretan.com/tools/assessment-tools/soulscreen/

Other unconscious thoughts follow: I need to play a role in order to get what I need to be fully myself; I need to get more so that I can be more."[27] So, although our lives often succumb to the direction of the external compass of our social self—the outside measure, we yearn to be guided more authentically from the compass within, by our essential self—the inside measure.

The essential self falls in love (the social self will try to tap into fear by dismissing this as infatuation, warning that the object of our desires is flawed, dangerous, unreliable, and sometimes unattractive). The essential self wants to make the world a better place, but the social self is more focused on ego gratification. The social self seeks to motivate with fear, and those who seek to motivate others deliberately tap into the fears of the social self. The embers of inspiration perpetually burn within the essential self, and those who seek to inspire others fan those embers into flames. The essential self unapologetically embraces idealism, seldom flinching when subjected to the criticism received from the social selves of others. Our best selves live in the essential self— and the Dark Triad personality lives in the social self.

The most frequently seen leadership style is one that emanates principally from the social self, typically characterized by ambition, determination, competition, aggression, and goal attainment, and this results in the

27 Eckhart Tolle, *A New Earth: Awakening to Your Life's Purpose*, Penguin; Reprint edition, January 30, 2008, Chapter 4, Role-playing: The Many Faces of the Ego, page 109.

dismal data on self-interested leadership referred to earlier. Living a life that is inspiring, and that inspires others, requires that we listen to the essential self at least as often as we listen to the social self—hearing and respecting both. In other words, inspiring leadership, and being inspired, flows from joy more than success; from the essential self more than the social self. This is why so many people give up their corporate lives in exchange for the freedom, fulfillment, independence, and the pursuit of their dreams that beckon to them from the entrepreneurial life.

MOTIVATION

As illustrated in the example of the pharmaceutical company referred to earlier, motivation is something we *do* to people. It consists of a combination of two pressure points: fear and material rewards (or punishments). Motivation is seldom about the other person, but more often about *me*. I need to meet my corporate objectives, so I will *motivate* my staff by hiring a consulting firm who will train them to *align individual performance with corporate goals*. If they do so, then I will meet *my corporate objectives*. Motivation is largely an attempt to alter or control the behavior of others, raise performance standards, change attitudes or beliefs or exploit capacity—

in other words, the Machiavellian aspect of the Dark Triad personality. When we come from this position, we are working principally on the *social self*, tapping into, and exploiting, the fears of the person we are trying to motivate, relying on shaming, bribing, rewarding, threatening, or pressuring—all of which trigger the primal fear instincts. When planning an initiative, for example, we often ask, "How can I motivate this group to reach the targets I have set for them?"

Another motivational technique is to reward or punish an individual with the prospect of being "in" (reward) or "out" (punishment) of favor—("Not only did you fail to make your bonus, but you belong to the rest of the deadbeat group who also failed!"). When we use fear in this way to coach or lead, the person being coached or led (I use these terms loosely in this case) experiences anxiety and stress.

Most of our modern theory of marketing is based on motivation and is deployed in almost every part of society: "Buy my lotion or you will be ugly." Our religions are often based on fear: "Join my faith or you will go to hell." Politics run this way, too: "Vote for me or the other guy will raise your taxes." The way we run organizations often falls into this same pattern: "Do what I say, or we'll fire you." And, of course, performance management has long followed this path: "Reach these goals, and we will reward you; miss them, and we will punish you." Even some parents use motivation this way: "Do what I say or I'll punish you." Motivation is extrinsic, relies on fear and material rewards or punishments, and is targeted at the level of the social self—the ego or the personality. Motivation often gets things done—but at a price. And that price is often resentment, anger, lack of trust, and reprisal. Fear-based motivation is why 71 percent of employees were either "actively looking for new job opportunities" or had the topic on their minds "always, often or sometimes" at work, as stated in the report mentioned earlier in this chapter.

INSPIRATION

I do not wish to suggest that motivation is unimportant. If the room you are in catches fire, I will motivate you to get out of it quickly! Instead, what I'm suggesting is that we have become experts at motivation, we have built theories of leadership and human resource policies around the fear-based system called motivation, and we have learned how to do this extraordinarily well. Our leadership theories and human resource policy manuals are filled with motivation-driven compensation plans, models, and directives, and, as we have seen, they are not working very well. Yet, we have no such equivalent expertise in inspiration. Worse, we use the terms motivation and inspiration interchangeably as if they meant the same thing ("I want to be motivated and inspired!"), and yet, as I will explain, motivation and inspiration are almost exact opposites.

Inspiration is intrinsic. Unlike motivation, it does not come from fear, but from love. It is not about me—it is almost always exclusively about *you*. Great leaders and coaches want to inspire others to grow, to accomplish *their* objectives, to shine, to reach *their* potential and splendor. Any rewards for these inspiring coaches and leaders come from the joy they experience when helping others to reach *their* own goals or become larger as fully-realized human beings. Therefore, inspiration is an act of love and service to others, whereas motivation is self-centered—think the Machiavellianism, narcissism, and psychopathy of the Dark Triad personality. Like almost everyone, you can likely recall a mentor, teacher, coach, family member, or leader who made a difference in your life—these were all people who *loved* and inspired you. They would not have devoted the time and resources they did to you if they had not felt that way, and to this day, their loving legacy warms your heart. Motivation can be useful sometimes to get small (and occasionally important) things done in the short term; inspiration is more effective in getting big things done over the long term. Inspiration is aimed at the essential self—the soul of another, and is most often generated from within; the inspirer is merely the facilitator of the inspired—this is the essence of a great mentor.

As I stated earlier, life is about relationships—with each other, and with everything around us. Every choice we make, and everyone with whom we choose to connect, is the result of our searching for a loving and inspiring relationship. We join companies that inspire us and quit them when they no longer do so. We fall in love with people who inspire us and end the relationship when they no longer do so. We smell a flower, go to a movie, listen to our favorite music and eat at our favorite restaurants, all because we have a relationship with each of these things that inspire us. When this is no longer true and we become uninspired, we end the relationship. We pursue inspiring relationships and we distance ourselves from uninspiring ones. This is the key to our relationships with people. It's true in business, and it's true in the rest of our lives.

HOW TO DISTINGUISH MOTIVATION FROM INSPIRATION

- Motivation is based on fear; inspiration is based on love.
- Motivation is based on a need for each other; inspiration is based on love for each other.

- Motivation is driven by the social self; inspiration is energized by the essential self.
- Motivation is based on *me*, on serving *my* needs; inspiration is based on *you*, on serving *your* needs.
- Motivation is doing something you probably wouldn't do if you didn't have to; inspiration is doing something you would do anyway.
- Motivation is a "push"; inspiration is a "pull."
- Motivation is an idea you go after; inspiration is an idea that goes after you.
- Motivation is lighting a fire *under* someone; Inspiration is lighting a fire *within* someone.

The fact that we use the terms "motivation" and "inspiration" interchangeably suggests that our understanding of the difference is weak, and because of this, we are not clear about when to use the one or the other.

It is time to become as expert and practiced at inspiring each other as we have become at motivating each other. Our capacity for leadership and coaching— in fact, any means by which we enhance the spirit of others—will become raised when we develop inspiring processes, make organizations and experiences inspiring, and focus on and grow our expertise in being inspiring for others—in every aspect of our lives.

FIGURE 3: Maslow and Higher Ground Leadership®

Most people are familiar with Abraham Maslow's five-level Hierarchy of Needs, which he originally proposed in a paper published in 1943 entitled "A Theory of Human Motivation" and more fully expressed in his 1954 book *Motivation and Personality*. His work is usually interpreted as a pyramid, but Maslow never actually created a pyramid, nor did he say that each level was separate from the others. In his later work, he explored additional aspirations, although these were not part of his original five-level model.

The Fear-Based Needs

1. **Physiological Needs:** These include the primal needs of air, water, food, shelter, sex, and other physical needs. Meeting these needs is a prerequisite for progressing to higher needs.

2. **Safety Needs:** If the primal physiological needs are relatively satisfied, the needs that then become dominant arise out of the fear of being unsafe. These needs include health, well-being, and personal and financial safety. Job security also falls within this need category.

3. **Belonging Needs:** When physiological and safety needs are fulfilled, the third priority of human needs becomes social. These belonging needs, which are an interpersonal aspect of Maslow's hierarchy, are motivated by the fear of being deprived of emotionally based relationships, such as with family, friends, and social groups. Failure to meet these needs can result in depression, loneliness, and anxiety.

4. **Esteem Needs:** All humans have a need to be respected, valued, and accepted by others. Maslow made a distinction between respect from others (a "lower" need) and self-respect (a "higher" need). Not having these needs met may lead to an inferiority complex, weakness, and helplessness.

All of these first four needs are ego-based, emanating from the social self, and motivated by a fear of deficiency. Fear drives motivation.

A shift occurs as we move from fear-based motivations of the first four levels of the hierarchy above to the next four levels, to the aspirational desires (not needs). These are aspirations that we love—and that inspire us; they are listed below. We are drawn to the pursuit of personal growth, guiding us toward the aspirational desires we love, and this always emanates from the essential self. Love generates inspiration. We love what inspires us.

The Love-Based Desires

While Maslow did not build any additional levels in his original model beyond the fifth one (self-actualization), I describe below an expanded projection of his later work. I am fully aware that I am taking intellectual liberties with my proposition, and I do so with acknowledgment and deference to a brilliant, pioneering thinker.

1. **Cognitive Desires:** Maslow believed that humans have an innate curiosity and a deep desire for personal growth and knowledge. The cognitive desires of the essential self are rooted in a love of the world—curiosity, learning, exploration, discovery, and creativity—all inspiring us to understand. This cognitive desire is characterized by a love of openness to new ideas and concepts, a desire to grow, to seek knowledge, learning, and wisdom, and when this is unfulfilled, it can lead to personal frustration and a confused sense of one's place in the bigger scheme of things.

2. **Esthetic Desires:** The essential self seeks beauty over ugliness. We love beauty, harmony, and order, and we love being surrounded by beauty, and when we are, we are inspired. The essential self is nourished in the presence and beauty of nature, art, and people—infused by the beauty offered by the world. This desire creates a feeling of intimacy with all that is graceful and elegant. This is inspiration.

3. **Self-Actualization Desires:** Maslow clearly described self-actualization as the instinctual desire of humans to realize their full potential. "What a man can be, he must be," Maslow said. This desire, when fulfilled, contributes to the greater good and generates feelings of personal inspiration.

4. **Self-Transcendence Desires:** Maslow believed that the next step for the actualized person was a desire to give themselves to higher goals that transcend the self, relating with others and the world in an altruistic and spiritual way. He wrote, "Transcendence refers to the very highest and most inclusive or holistic levels of human consciousness, behaving and relating, as ends rather than means, to oneself, to significant others, to human beings in general, to other species, to nature, and to the cosmos."[28] For most people, this is not so much a fully realized aspiration, but rather a pilgrimage. It is an inspiring condition of oneness (see Chapter 4),

---

28 *Farther Reaches of Human Nature*, Abraham H. Maslow and Bertha G. Maslow, 1993, ISBN-13: 978-0140194708, p. 269.

a deep acceptance of, and love for, the mysteries of the Universe—what some refer to as mysticism.

From this description, it can be seen that the first four levels of the hierarchy are needs—not desires—calibrated externally (success), driven by a fear that these needs may not be met, rooted in the social self, and highly susceptible to, and likely to generate, fear-based motivation.

As we cross over from the first four fear-based needs to the four love-based desires, things change. We shift from a focus on the social self to a focus on the essential self, from me to you, from fear to love, and from motivation to inspiration.

In the strict academic sense, perhaps the pursuit of "leadership" is an unteachable and unattainable holy grail. With all of the investments we've made, all the teaching, seminars, consulting, research, and writing that have been conducted into the subject, we seem to be no further ahead than we were 40 years ago, when the "leadership industry" was founded. A clear-thinking person will realize the fruitlessness of continuing to do the same thing while expecting different results. Saint Augustine said, "What then is time? If no one asks me, I know what it is. If I wish to explain it to him who asks, I do not know." Leadership is the same: we all think that we know what it is, but when asked to define it or describe it, there are as many answers as respondents. How can we teach that which we cannot describe?

We are in a new era in which our traditional models and metaphors for leadership have become obsolete. Unless we rethink our approach to leadership, we risk losing an entire generation of employees (and future leaders), who will be so disenchanted with the corporate world that they will seek alternatives. Today's organizations and their leaders are ill prepared for the shift that is occurring in our society. Structure, hierarchy, pay levels, endless (and boring) meetings, assessments, PowerPoint® presentations, bureaucracy, and the like are asphyxiating for the new wave of employees who are creative, digital, socially and environmentally conscious, independent thinkers. They are free spirits who don't think of work and play as separate domains any more than they separate their work and personal or social life. For them, everything is connected—it is one (see the following chapter). They don't need to be led—they want to be inspired. Understanding the power and advantage of inspiration over motivation will bring about a transformation in our appreciation of what leadership is and regenerate corporate cultures so that they become magnets for brilliant people and passionate customers.[29]

Harry Gordon Selfridge said, "The boss drives people; the leader coaches them. The boss depends on authority; the leader on goodwill. The boss inspires fear; the leader inspires enthusiasm. The boss says I; The leader says WE.

---

29 See also the work of Martin Seligman (*Positive Psychology*) and Mihály Csíkszentmihályi (*Flow*).

The boss fixes the blame for the breakdown; the leader fixes the breakdown. The boss says, GO; the leader says, Let's GO!"

Teaching "leadership" may in itself have become obsolete, because most people do not want to be led—they want to be inspired. Teams that are led will do as they're told; teams that are inspired will do whatever it takes. Many uninspiring organizations have highly skilled "leaders" at the helm, but those organizations will never realize their full potential until they focus on growing their capacity to inspire. Inspiring organizations are a magnet for the best talent, customers, and vendors. Leadership is simply a subset of inspiration. And we *love* inspiring people and inspiring organizations.

FOUR

From Separateness to Oneness

FROM CLASSICAL TO QUANTUM LEADERSHIP

Classical physics invites us to measure matter and energy through observable human experience, analyzing the separate parts, and this is largely the way we explain science and technology today. Newtonian mechanics, electrodynamics, thermodynamics, and the laws of special and general relativity form the toolbox of scientists practicing classical physics. This way of seeing things works well with physical objects at the level of atoms, molecules, and larger, but at the subatomic level, these tools and laws become ineffective, failing to provide a correct description of life. Using these crude tools, we mistakenly believe that all observable objects are separate from each other. So we see competitors, colleagues, vendors, customers, media, unions, regulators, and shareholders as separate entities and as separate from us. But when we investigate the essence of matter, from which all physical objects are made, we find that everything is one, not separate, and that we need different scientific tools with which to measure this "oneness." This includes quantum theory and relativity.

Without going down a scientific rabbit hole here, we have learned that the theories and models of classical physics do not adequately describe the universe, and that, in reality, the newer science of quantum physics informs us that there are no separate entities—everything is connected—and that separateness is an illusion. Within quantum theory, there is a concept called "quantum entanglement," which describes the phenomenon where a pair of subatomic particles cannot be described independently of each other—even when those particles are many kilometers apart—but instead, can only be described as a whole. And just as intriguing, the act of measuring one thing determines the possible quantum state of another—the so-called Heisenberg Principle, to which I will refer later.

HOW WE GOT TO SEPARATENESS

It doesn't really matter whether you are a creationist or an evolutionist, or even if you don't believe in anything at all—whatever your personal explanation for the origins of the universe may be, you will probably agree that it was born out of *something* that was, at one time, one. The creationist believes that a few days passed between "the beginning," when there was oneness, and the introduction of a human, and that a few more days passed before the fall of Adam and Eve. The evolutionist believes billions of years passed between the oneness of the beginning and the evolution of humans, but both refer to a mystery—the moment of oneness from which all this emerged. From there, the world evolved, and your personal philosophy will define how you interpret these events. The creationists and the evolutionists disagree about *how* the world began, but agree that at the beginning, there was stillness—or oneness.

In those early prehistoric, prescientific days, we believed everything was one. Partly this was because we couldn't see anything beyond our immediately observable environment. Even though we did not communicate in ways to which we can relate today, the myths and legends by which we explained our existence were universally shared—similar to the way particles share information in quantum entanglement. For example, the circular concept of time was the belief shared by Native Americans, ancient Hebrews, the Inuit of the Arctic, the Maoris of New Zealand, the Bantu of Southern Africa, the Aboriginals of Australia, and many others. How could they have known and shared the same perspective and understanding of time being circular without any means of communication, unless they were one—in other words entangled at the quantum level? We believed in the same concept of time because our existence was rooted in oneness.

It is understandable that we have now come to view the world as if everything were separate, and this completely revised perspective has evolved over millennia. Twenty-five hundred years ago, the Greek philosophers, among them Aristotle, Plato, and Socrates, were some of the first to reject the early explanations of the phenomena they saw around them, which were based on myth, mystery and magic, in favor of more rational explanations. They began to use reason and observation to reveal the true nature of the world as they saw it, and they used rational argument to explain and promote their views. They showed us how to separate the parts that make up oneness, so that we could more easily understand the world. On these shoulders stood philosophers, mathematicians, and scientists like Copernicus, Galileo, Machiavelli, Newton, Descartes, Hume, Hobbes, and others who gave us the early versions of what we now call the "scientific method," which we have since refined as we continue to deepen our embrace of separateness.

Our entire education system is built on the notion of separateness. We teach different subjects, models, and theories; we grade students and stream them by separating them into learning abilities and performance; we provide access to higher education by separating students using their GPA or GMAT scores; we even educate separately through private and public systems, and the entire conventional teaching paradigm is built on the platform of the scientific method, a methodology that teaches complex ideas by separating them into the smallest parts so they can be more easily understood. And so we enter the world with an operational mindset that has been trained over many years to look for separateness. In fact, we have undergone changes to the hardwiring of our brains over the last several centuries that have programmed us to think in terms of separateness rather than oneness.

THE FALLACY OF SEPARATENESS

Although the physical objects that we can observe appear to have separate boundaries, this is not the case. To make this more concrete, let's use a specific example: I could be rude, curt, and demeaning to you, and then turn around and, within earshot, be graceful, charming, and elegant with your neighbor, and with our respective eyes, we would all see this and describe it as two separate acts.

But at the quantum level, the level of subatomic particles, it is very different. If a particle is split and one half remains where we are and the other half is transported to a distant location, both will retain the same properties, regardless of their distance from each other. In another phenomenon, known as the Heisenberg Principle referred to earlier, the state of that particle will not be known until it is observed—the act of observation being the agent of the change. Let's go back to our example: I could be rude, curt, and demeaning to you, and then turn around and, within earshot, be graceful, charming, and elegant with your neighbor, and while we might all observe this as two separate acts, in truth, each party receiving and experiencing the different styles of communication will be affected by both, and therefore, to a greater or lesser degree, both parties will experience the separate behaviors as one. While our churlish behavior may be directed at another, we will vicariously experience it too.

EMBRACING ONENESS

Our approach to running organizations and leadership (and just about everything else too) continues to use a "classical" approach, even though we now understand that this will not give us the answers we need and that we need to use new (old, actually, but newly discovered) "quantum" tools.

Today, our culture is rooted in the concept of separateness. We organize every aspect of our lives into tiny segments of separateness. I described earlier the example of separateness in academia. We also have the tools to separate into categories and specialties in almost any field, including religion, politics, beliefs, gender, income, status, generations (X, Y, millennials, etc.), demographics, skin color, ethnic background, countries, health and well-being, education, income, and more. We deepen this separateness-thinking daily as "big data," and digital algorithms take an increasingly central position in influencing our lives.

In companies, we practice separateness by creating specializations, functional departments, corporate hierarchies and bureaucracies, tenure and seniority, ageism, union and non-union, tenured and non-tenured, divisions, markets, and many subtle and insidious methods to separate one group from another.

The outdated approach of classical physics, and some aspects of "the scientific method," is what we have been using to study and teach leadership—as a subject consisting of separate parts—leaders, followers, organizations, contexts, goals, and more. We have even succumbed to the false belief that behavior displayed and exhibited within an organization is separate from, and sometimes not even appropriate for, life outside the organization—for example, at home. As I described in Chapter 2, we behave with one set of learned attributes at work, and an entirely different, and separate, set of attributes at home. We falsely believe that defeating our competition is a separate act that will not affect us, or that self-dealing will benefit me while not affecting the whole, or that CEO pay can be hundreds of times larger than the average employee's earnings without repercussions, or that my organization can poison the environment without affecting the people who live in it. But these, and many other examples of separateness, are an illusion—everything is connected and everything is one.

There is a growing awareness, even if the practice lags behind, that inclusion leads to inspiration and oneness. Separateness—when we are excluded or made to feel separate—is uninspiring and painful, leading to the epidemic of disaffected employees and dysfunctional organizations. Gandhi said, "No culture can live if it attempts to be exclusive," and Jesse Jackson said, "When everyone is included, everyone wins"—advice for corporate leaders to live by.

Thomas Merton wrote, "The deepest level of communication is not communication, but communion. It is wordless. It is beyond words. It is beyond speech. It is beyond concept. Not that we discover a new unity, but we discover an old unity. My dear brothers and sisters, we are already one. But we imagine we are not. And what we have to recover is our original unity. What we have to be, is what we are."[30]

---

30 Thomas Merton, *The Asian Journal of Thomas Merton*, 1975, New Directions Books, ISBN-13: 978-0811205702

Sometimes, what prevents us from seeing the whole is our hurry to implement and move on to the next project. It is quicker, and sometimes even easier, to view the object in front of us—often a person—as separate from everything else, as if it were a project that we need to get done *now*. As Ralph Waldo Emerson reminds us, "Adopt the pace of nature: her secret is patience." As our pace of life (and brain functions) is quickened by new technologies, it can take a little longer to slow our thought processes down sufficiently to allow us to consider how the decision we are about to make may ripple into other parts of our world. No decision is ever made in isolation, even if we believe otherwise.

The connections are everywhere—at the level of the universe, and at the level of the tiniest subatomic iota, and everything in between. Amazon introduces a new way to sell books, and traditional bookstores go out of business. A supervisor harangues her employee, and both take their anger, frustration, and resentment home and share it there. An employee gives poor service to a customer, and the customer tells 11 other people not to shop there anymore. (According to the White House Office of Consumer Affairs, dissatisfied customers will tell between 9 and 15 people about their experiences. Around 13 percent of dissatisfied customers tell more than 20 people). A company exploits loopholes to avoid paying taxes, and the plummeting customer respect and loyalty that result adversely affect its sales. If we squeeze one part of the balloon, we cannot avoid affecting the rest. There are no separate waves, just one ocean; no separate water, just infinite numbers of subatomic particles working in "quantum entanglement."

In the quantum organization, leaders (and everyone else) consider the whole, knowing that there are no actions without reactions. Life is energy, and everything we do has both intended and unintended consequences. Every decision we make needs to be filtered through that awareness—the awareness that there are wider implications beyond the obvious for all of our actions. As I wrote in my book *ONE: The Art and Practice of Conscious Leadership:*

> "Whenever we experience pain or sadness, it is because we have become separated from what, or whom, we love. And whenever we are inspired and joyful, it is because we are one with what, or whom, we love. All human challenges and successes can be explained through this awareness."[31]

This also explains why some organizations are great and some are mediocre. The ability to understand the power of oneness is one of the greatest single opportunities for a leader to transform a corporate culture into an inspiring one. When we separate functions, departments, teams,

---

31 *ONE: The Art and Practice of Conscious Leadership* by Lance Secretan, The Secretan Center Inc., 2006, ISBN-13: 978-0973311556, page 11

hierarchies, markets, divisions, we become uninspiring. And when we see these as one, align the organization behind a unified, inspiring dream (see Chapter 8 for more on this), remove hierarchies and distinctions, and become *one* team—then we are positioned to build levels of greatness that are distinctive and remarkable. Inclusion leads to oneness, and oneness is inspiring because it helps us to understand that we are a part of the whole and of something bigger than "just me" or my department. We all are more inspired by a higher purpose, a larger idea, connection, and collaboration than our own little territorial box. There is passion, magic, and excellence in *oneness*.

We have the Internet of Everything. Now it is time to work on the Inclusion of Everyone—oneness.

FIVE

From Engagement to Inspiration

In the 1970s, Dr. George Gallup, founder of the eponymous polling company Gallup Inc., observed that less than half of North American employees were satisfied with their work, and the data was even worse in Western Europe, Africa, Latin America, and the Far East. In those days, he was measuring employee satisfaction, which, of course, is a different thing from employee engagement. Employee satisfaction typically measures the level of "happiness" experienced by employees with their working conditions, while engagement attempts to measure the level of discretionary "passion" they are prepared to invest in their work.

At the same time, Dr. Donald O. Clifton, a psychologist and professor at Nebraska University, was studying the causes of success in business and academia. In 1988, he merged his company, Selection Research Incorporated, with Dr. Gallup's firm, bringing together Gallup's polling expertise and Clifton's emphasis on Positive Psychology, the science of what makes people flourish. In the 1990s, Gallup developed the first iteration of their famous Q^{12} Survey, so named because it contained just 12 survey questions. It has remained the gold standard in measuring employee engagement, a broader measure than employee satisfaction, because it attempts to measure the level of discretionary energy and emotional commitment an employee is willing to invest in the organization.

Forty years after Dr. Gallup's original research, billions of dollars invested, and more than 30 suppliers providing $1.5 billion of engagement surveys each year to the world, the results haven't budged. Today, roughly 30 percent of US employees are "engaged," 52 percent are disengaged, and 18 percent are actively disengaged. Paraphrasing a metaphor used by Mark Crowley in an article in *Fast Company* magazine,[32] we can see just how broken the situation is: if these perennially dismal

---

32 "Gallup's Workplace Jedi On How To Fix Our Employee Engagement Problem," Mark C. Crowley, *Fast Company*: https://www.fastcompany.com/3011032/ gallups-workplace-jedi-on-how-to-fix-our-employee-engagement-problem

levels of employee engagement were the experience of a rowing eight, three rowers would be paddling like crazy, four would be casually taking in the scenery, and one would be actively trying to sink the boat!

Globally, the data is just as dismal—34 percent are engaged, 48 percent are disengaged, and 18 percent are actively disengaged. Just to be clear, that means that nearly one in five employees is trying to sabotage your company! This level of disengagement translates into between $450-550 billion in lost productivity, and the cost per employee to gather this information can be as high as $400[33]—which proves that measuring something doesn't necessarily improve it.

All this raises endless questions—for example: Does increased employee engagement cause improved corporate success, or is it the other way around? There is scant research supporting engagement as a key contributor to corporate performance, but much research showing that successful companies have more engaged employees!

Are the most engaged employees the most productive? Research by Leadership IQ reveals that in 42 percent of organizations, low performers are actually *more engaged* than high and middle performers. And there seems to be little agreement on what factors lead to improved employee engagement. Edward Lawler III, a

---

33 "Present And Future Of Employee Engagement, and The News Is Bad, Really Bad," Work911.com: http://work911.com/issues/Employee_Engagement_-_Boon_ Or_Bust/

distinguished professor of business at the University of Southern California (USC) Marshall School of Business, writing in *Forbes* in an article appropriately titled "An Idiot's Guide to Employee Engagement,"[34] points out that

- money has a significant positive impact on engagement
- performing well leads to engagement, not the other way around
- there is no single measure, because people value different things
- individual expectations, when met and rewarded, lead to higher engagement
- job satisfaction may mean employees have no desire to leave the organization, but not necessarily that they will strive to produce more.

In short, employee engagement surveys don't tell us much, and extensive research suggests they don't have any impact on performance either.

Furthermore, if an organization brags about being in the top 10 percentile, what does this mean, since only 30 percent of employees surveyed are engaged?

---

34 "An Idiot's Guide to Employee Engagement," Edward E. Lawler III, *Forbes*: https://www.forbes.com/sites/edwardlawler/2012/11/08/ an-idiots-guide-to-employee-engagement/#7e859ead7570

THE EMPLOYEE ENGAGEMENT PARADOX

There is a paradox with a survey such as the Gallup Q^{12}. As we have seen, we have made no progress over the years in improving engagement scores, yet we keep measuring engagement—another example of the Bellwether Effect and the extreme dissonance that can result. In the world of measuring employee satisfaction or engagement, Gallup is the mother of all Bellwether Effect forerunners, with a database of 25 million survey takers in over 100 countries—a marketing and forerunner juggernaut that is so deeply embedded in modern management practice that threshold *n* is now a speck in the rearview mirror. It is a marketing phenomenon.[35] As others have opined, Gallup sells surveys, not solutions, and it therefore makes sense to market the notion that measuring will impact results. Yet, as I have shown above, the data tells a different story.

Another result of the Bellwether Effect is how engagement surveys become a way for human resource professionals to demonstrate that they are doing "something strategic." In his 1996 book *Human Resource Champions*, David Ulrich identified four roles that human resource professionals must play in the modern organization in order to become more relevant: employee champion,

---

35 Gallup's 2016 Q^{12} Meta-Analysis Report: http://news.gallup.com/
reports/191489/q12-meta-analysis-report-2016.aspx

administrative expert, change agent, and strategic partner. He wrote that "employee champions deliver competent and committed employees, administrative experts deliver efficient HR practices, change agents deliver capacity for change in individual behavior and organizational culture, and strategic partners deliver business results." Some human resource professionals have been caught like deer in the headlights as they strive to bend employee engagement surveys to this model, thus, through association, attempting to justify and prove their professional relevance. But still no annual incremental change in engagement scores occurs.

Patty McCord, former Netflix Chief Talent Officer, shares these five tenets that helped Netflix reinvent HR:

1. Hire, reward, and tolerate only fully formed adults
2. Tell the truth about performance
3. Managers own the job of creating great teams
4. Leaders own the job of creating the company culture
5. Good talent managers think like businesspeople and innovators first and like HR people last[36]

Although often dressed up differently, engagement surveys are typically deployed as a means to improve organizational performance, not enhance the lives of employees. This can often be viewed by employees as

---

36 "How Netflix Reinvented HR," Patty McCord, *Harvard Business Review*: https://hbr.org/2014/01/how-netflix-reinvented-hr

exploitive and manipulative—an effort to maximize output without additional cost—the Dark Triad again. Employees quickly see through this, and it can often grate with them instead of inspiring them, thus achieving exactly the opposite results from those intended.

THE EMPLOYEE IS THE NEW CUSTOMER

We have been urged for years to place the customer at the top of our list of organizational priorities. There has been much good work done in this field, and those who excel in customer service have reaped great benefits. But the reality today is that this equation isn't sufficient in itself. The purpose of any organization is to provide maximum value to customers and/or other stakeholders. The people who do that are employees. If we need to prioritize at all, we might put the employee as the top priority, because if we inspire employees, they will inspire customers—and, of course, everyone else. Therefore, *the employee is the new customer*. This is how Virgin, Southwest Airlines, Starbucks, The Boston Beer Company, The Container Store, EllisDon, HCL Technologies,[37] New Belgium Brewing, and others have

---

37 The CEO of India-based HCL Technologies, Vineet Nayar, wrote the book *Employees First, Customers Second: Turning Conventional Management Upside Down*, Harvard Business Review Press, 2010, ISBN-13: 978-1422139066

become extraordinarily successful. Southwest Airlines even extends this ranking: employees first, customers second, shareholders third. Ritz-Carlton refers to its employees as "Ladies and Gentlemen," and the company's motto is, "We are Ladies and Gentlemen serving Ladies and Gentlemen."

Alibaba.com has become the world's largest online business-to-business global trading marketplace, with 2.5 million and 14 million registered users in its international and Chinese domestic marketplaces respectively. Its online sales and profits surpassed all U.S. retailers (including Walmart, Amazon, and eBay) combined since 2015. The company's founder, Jack Ma, believes that one of the main purposes of Alibaba is to provide a community where employees can have fun working together and pursue their dreams with minimal bureaucracy and politics. Ma recently painted a vivid image of his ideal work environment for Alibaba's employees as follows:

- **Blue Sky** (蓝蓝的天): Processes, systems, and decisions need to be open and transparent. There's nothing that should be hidden from employees. We should be transparent.
- **Solid Ground** (踏实的大地): Everything we do should be honest, ethical and contribute to the welfare of the society. The company should be on solid financial ground so employees won't worry about the financial future of the company.

- **Free-flowing Ocean** (流动的大海): Talent must be allowed to rotate jobs across subsidiaries and departments.
- **Green Forest** (绿色的森林): Conducive conditions for continued innovation.
- **Harmonious Community** (和谐的社区): Peers with shared values and simple interpersonal relationships.

"The ultimate objective of such a community," he continues, "is to offer employees a work environment to grow, contribute, and live out their dreams. Bureaucracy, secrecy, and stagnation are all attributes that inhibit employees, and the company must actively seek out these behaviors and destroy them."[38] Alibaba is a company that puts employees first and has built a global success story through the energy of inspired employees who feel a part of the whole.

In healthcare, the buzzword *du jour* is "evidence-based, patient-centered healthcare." Considering the first half of this phrase, in cases of pain, nausea, or fatigue, and some other conditions, it has been widely documented that placebos are often more effective than drugs. In fact, Dr. Ted J. Kaptchuk, a professor of medicine at Harvard Medical School and director of the Harvard-wide Program in Placebo Studies and the Therapeutic Encounter (PiPS) at Beth Israel Deaconess Medical Center

---

38 "Alibaba.com: A Smiling Community with a Dream," Jack Ma: https://im.ft-static.com/content/images/c6aba388-74a6-11db-bc76-0000779e2340.pdf

in Boston, has conducted studies in which even people who knew that they were receiving a placebo still reported significant improvements in their symptoms compared to a parallel test group who received nothing! In fact, another study suggests that more than half the effectiveness of a drug is due to the placebo effect.[39] So evidence-based healthcare, though useful, is not the only requirement to achieve wellness. The science of evidence-based healthcare is compelling, but it isn't sufficient on its own—we must also take into account the mysterious subtlety of the placebo.

And regarding the second half of the phrase, if we incessantly tell nurses that the patient is the most important component of the healthcare system, and we drill it into him or her every day for 30 years, is it any wonder that he or she may feel a level of diminished self-esteem? I often tell my healthcare clients that despite many claims to the contrary, there is no shortage of nurses in healthcare. But there is a real shortage of *places where nurses want to work.* So it appears that the evidence isn't the only important thing in healthcare, and neither is the patient. A better phrase, then, to describe quality healthcare might be, "people-centered, results-oriented healthcare." In this way, by treating employees as people, we would be elevating their value to equal status

---

39 "Altered Placebo and Drug Labeling Changes the Outcome of Episodic Migraine Attacks," Slavenka Kam-Hansen, Moshe Jakubowski, John M. Kelley, Irving Kirsch, David C. Hoaglin, Ted J. Kaptchuk and Rami Burstein, *Science Translational Medicine:* http://stm.sciencemag.org/content/6/218/218ra5

with *all people*, including clinicians, patients, outside vendors, unions, regulators, and others. This would recognize the fact that it takes *all people* to make an organization work, and in doing so, we could change the entire culture of healthcare. Instead of making clinicians feel "second" to patients, we could inspire them by fully honoring them, just as we do for all people.

According to research by Eric Garton and Michael Mankins, partners at Bain & Company, inspired employees are 2¼ times more productive than satisfied employees.[40] The comparison looks like this:

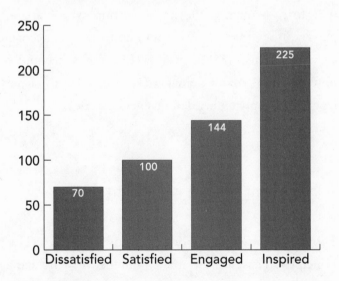

FIGURE 4: Inspired Employees Compared to Engaged Employees

---

40 "Engaging Your Employees is Good, but Don't Stop There," Emma Luxton, *World Economic Forum*: https://www.weforum.org/agenda/2016/03/engaging-your-employees-is-good-but-don-t-stop-there/

I have heard it said, "I always give 100 percent at work: 10 percent Monday, 23 percent Tuesday, 40 percent Wednesday, 22 percent Thursday, 5 percent Friday!" If you were starting a new company—wouldn't you be looking for, and wanting to grow, inspired employees instead of engaged ones? Why have we agreed to set such a low bar by settling merely for engaged employees? Surely the standard for which we should be striving is something much more ambitious—inspired employees. And not just 30 percent of them either. In fact, research shows that on average, only 15 percent of a company's workforce—roughly one in seven employees—are "A players," or "stars."[41] We continue to use engagement surveys because the Bellwether Effect has become so powerful that many managers do not dare to depart from this deeply embedded business practice.

THE CASTLE® PRINCIPLES

Those familiar with my work will know of The CASTLE® Principles. These were framed a number of years ago as a result of extensive research into what people found *uninspiring* about their work and their bosses (I use the

---

41 "The Best Companies Don't Have More Stars—They Cluster Them Together," Michael C. Mankins, *Insights*, Bain & Company: http://www.bain.com/ publications/articles/the-best-companies-dont-have-more-stars-hbr.aspx

pejorative term "boss" knowingly here). The responses were very clear. They detested:

a. Cowards
b. Phony people
c. Self-serving and selfish people
d. Liars
e. Those who ruled with fear, and
f. Idiots—incompetent people

From here, it was a straightforward matter of searching for the opposites of these and testing whether they would provide a compact list of characteristics for which people yearn, find inspiring, and admire and love. Six reciprocal values emerged:

a. Courage
b. Authenticity
c. Service
d. Truthfulness
e. Love
f. Effectiveness

Additionally, as we completed due diligence on the validity of these values, we found that they were not just yearned for, inspiring, and admired and loved at work—but across every aspect of people's lives.

And thus were born the CASTLE® Principles, CASTLE being the acronym for these six principles.

Today, there are hundreds of applications and uses for the CASTLE® Principles,[42] but in this context, I want to show how they can offer the basis for a superior alternative to traditional engagement surveys.

First, let's agree that checking in with each other is not a semi-annual or annual chore (more on this in the next chapter). It is an ongoing dialogue (*dialogue: noun: an exchange of ideas or opinions on a particular issue*) in which we learn, grow, and inspire. It consists of deep listening and also speaking—in that order.

Secondly, let's agree that for every individual, there is a tailored dialogue—one-size-fits-all surveys will not get us to an informed place from which we can build an inspiring culture.

Thirdly, we need to agree on the kinds of questions we want to ask under the broad heading of each of the CASTLE® Principles. One of the weaknesses of traditional engagement surveys is that they ask insipid questions, such as, "Do you have the materials and equipment to do your work right?" If there is any question at all about a subject as fundamental as this, much deeper problems are certain to exist. Any competent leadership team will ensure that the basics are provided for getting excellent work done—this should be considered "table stakes." Companies that can't even achieve this basic level of competence won't be able to stay in the game, or even survive. Can you imagine asking a player in a

---

42 A full description of the CASTLE® Principles can be found here: http://www.secretan.com/tools/media-and-learning-tools/castle-principles/

professional sports team, "Do you have the materials and equipment to do your work right?"

Deep questioning in regular dialogues requires questions of substance that pertain to the quality of relationships and how inspiring they are, because, as we have noted in Chapter 2, peak performance—at work, or anywhere else for that matter—depends on loving and inspiring connections and relationships.

What we want to learn is, "What is the quality of the relationship between the individual and their supervisor?," "What is the quality of the relationship between the individual and the organization as a whole?," and "What is the quality of the relationship between the employee and the output of that employee's work?" One can add additional dyads in certain cases, but these are the most critical. So, using the "Truthfulness" principle of the CASTLE® Principles, for example, we might want to ask:

- Does your leader tell the truth?
- Do you feel safe to tell the truth?
- Does your organization tell the truth?

This brings up another vital aspect of deep dialogue inquiry: traditional engagement surveys make a big deal about benchmarking a company's engagement survey data against their vast databases. If we ask a question such as "Does your leader tell the truth?," why does it matter if we benchmark this information against the responses of 25 million other people? Surely the only criterion that we should be considering is how each of our own employees *feels* about their individual leader? What 25 million other people feel about their leaders is irrelevant, and by the time the database has swelled to 25 million, comparisons become meaningless anyway. Even if the answer to this question is considered by anyone to be "inaccurate"—which would be a completely subjective opinion—it still describes the real perception of that particular respondent to that question and thus indicates an issue needing attention—or not. What is happening in other organizations is beside the point—this is a very personal question that pertains to relationships among people in our own organization.

Surveys can mislead us into a pursuit of fruitless objectives—like comparing ourselves to others. The point is *not* to compare the fact that my leader doesn't tell the truth and compare that data with 25 million other responses. The point is to work toward a new condition in which my leader *does* tell the truth, regardless of how our data compares to others—thus changing a relationship from a demoralizing one to an inspiring one.

I am often asked how the data generated by a survey containing questions such as the truthfulness one above compares to other surveys, particularly well-known engagement surveys. This raises some very interesting questions. First, there are no "other surveys like this"— it is a question that relies on, and compares, antiquated methodology to a tailored, deep questioning dialogue.

Secondly, as a leader, I am principally concerned with how my team members *feel* about *their* leader, *their* organization, and *their* work life, and if any of these, and other relationships, are not inspiring and top-notch, I want to take any action I can to improve the situation. Comparing to an outside organization is meaningless. There are no "quartiles" in this approach—it is an all-or-nothing approach—if it isn't excellent, then we need to work toward making it so, regardless of what anyone else is doing or saying.

As described in the Preface of this book, we need to be concerned with removing "interference." The equation is:

High Performance = potential − interference, or

$$HP=p-i$$

The purpose of deep dialogue using the CASTLE® Principles is to remove any interference that is obstructing an employee's opportunity to meet their full potential.

If we want to understand the temperature of our corporate climate in general and how inspired each individual employee is in particular, then we need to ask "edgy" questions—not insipid, vanilla ones. Below are some examples borrowed from the CASTLE® Organizational Survey.[43] A positive response to each of these statements will indicate a low level of interference.

---

43 You can test out the free CASTLE® Personal Survey here: www.secretan.com/tools/assessment-tools/castle-personal-survey/ and the paid CASTLE® Organizational Survey here: http://www.secretan.com/tools/assessment-tools/castle-organizational-survey/

COURAGE:

I see courage modeled every day by our leaders;
I am brave enough to ask the difficult questions at
work.

AUTHENTICITY:

Our organization's strategies and actions are in line
with our core values;
I am completely free to be myself at work.

SERVICE:

My leader actively supports me in achieving my
personal aspirations and dreams;
My work fills my life with meaning and fulfillment.

TRUTHFULNESS:

Truthfulness is honored as a top priority in this
organization;
I tell the truth in everything that I do at work.

LOVE:

I feel cared for and loved at work;
When I win, no one else loses.

EFFECTIVENESS:

My work makes an important contribution to
creating a better world;
We are among the best in the world at what we do.[44]

---

44 The complete CASTLE® Organizational Survey may be accessed here:
www.secretan.com/tools/assessment-tools/castle-organizational-survey/

The questions above are aimed at removing interference. Although formal surveys serve a purpose in certain circumstances, nothing compares to frequent, other-focused, deep dialogue that embraces the CASTLE® Principles at their core. For example, we could approach such questions by asking the following:

Am I being Courageous? Could I be more
Courageous?

Am I being Authentic? What would real Authenticity
in this situation look like?

Am I being of Service? Am I Serving the other?

Am I being Truthful? Am I being untruthful by
avoiding the Truth?

Am I being Loving? Will this person feel my Love
during and after this conversation?

Am I being Effective? How could I be more Effective?

In a culture that *lives* the CASTLE® Principles, where leaders are trusted and respected, where politics are rarely, if ever, present, and where people and their best interests count more than anything else, the best way to test the culture of the organization is to engage in frequent, authentic, deep dialogue. Keeping the CASTLE® Principles in one's heart and using them as a constant way to calibrate dialogue, actions, and decisions will elevate the corporate culture from one that may be engaged to one that will be *inspired*, because almost all of us want something deeper from our work life than we are experiencing. Then we can move from "30 percent engaged" to a journey where we aspire to be 100 percent inspired.

SIX

From Performance Appraisals to Constructive Check-Ins

THE PERFORMANCE APPRAISAL

I like to use a golden rule that I call the "Would-You-Do-This-With-Your-Spouse?" rule. For example, would you sit down once or twice a year with your spouse and embark on the following conversation: "Hi Honey! I'm glad we are having this conversation today. I'd like to go over a few things with you, including your key performance indicators, your budget, feedback from your colleagues, and set some objectives for the year ahead"? There are exactly 39 words in those three sentences, and my guess is that you would not get more than 10 of them out of your mouth before the blowback would be enough to push you backward out of the front door!

Why is this so? Because these words are demeaning, insulting, supercilious, one-sided, and offensive. Because it's advisable to treat an employee like a human being instead of a number. And one more thing: any self-respecting leader who pays attention at all and is close to the employee, checking in regularly and obtaining feedback, would already know the answers to all these questions.

I have argued for years that performance appraisals (also called performance reviews or performance management) are at best a subjective and intimidating process, and at worst a demoralizing drain on profits and productivity. Criticism of performance appraisal systems is considered heresy by some leaders, organizational development specialists, and HR professionals. But I see confirmation that the Bellwether Effect of performance appraisals creates painful dissonance because whenever I ask audiences if they like giving or receiving them, the answer is almost always 100 percent negative—another clear example of management persisting with a business process that everyone abhors despite the overwhelming evidence.

Performance appraisals were an affront from day one, but they are even less relevant in our contemporary context because the nature of work has changed so much. The linear, data-driven, metrics-based way of approaching people and business that our nineteenth- and twentieth-century forebears loved, is out of date. When how we work, live, and behave is distilled down to a five-point scale, there is no room left for creativity, innovation, fulfillment, meaning, collaboration, and dreams—the juice of inspiring organizations, and families. Now that we live in a world where we expect feedback within minutes from our recent Twitter or Instagram post, feedback that doesn't arrive until six or twelve months later seems quaintly archaic. Many people see the performance appraisal process as just one more time-wasting, bureaucratic chore that sucks time out of busy agendas and subjects people to an administrative grind that is uninspiring and filled with traps and dangers. Additionally, many HR processes, systems, and software are deeply linked to the annual performance ratings. Some industries, like healthcare in the U.S., for example, even mandate some form of annual performance review. Having a standardized, "objective" review of performance has been advised by experts in employment law in order to create a paper trail in the event of the need to terminate an employee for poor performance. Should we document our conversations with our spouses and ensure that there is a paper trail, just in case one of us should be considering a divorce in the future? No wonder the annual rating system arouses fear and loathing—it embodies the fear-based management approach that I have reviewed and criticized in Chapter 2.

Historically, traditional performance reviews have consisted of two components—accountability (How was your performance, and did you meet your goals over the last 12 months?) and development (What do you need to learn in order to grow, and where would you like your career to be heading?). Buried implicitly in both of these was the silent message, "Any merit increase you might receive will hinge greatly on this conversation." So we had a backward-looking assessment (accountability), a forward-looking scan (development), and a third element (pay increases) that muddled both. Of course, we have been professionally advised that it is wise to unlink the performance review from the salary review, but despite this caution, there can't be a person on the planet who doesn't think their performance rating will impact their salary, even if it isn't discussed at the time! As a result, the traditional performance review process made it nearly impossible to develop the necessary authentic conversations or trusting relationships in the workplace that lead to high performance.

The Bellwether Effect and the accompanying dissonance evident in the practice of performance appraisals have been pervasive: performance appraisals are viewed by 58 percent of organizations as ineffective (dissonance) and a waste of time, while a majority of organizations continue to make them a cornerstone of their performance management efforts (the Bellwether Effect), according to a study of 10,000 HR and business leaders in 140 countries by Bersin by Deloitte.[45] Researchers report that 90 percent of performance appraisals are painful and ineffective and don't improve performance and 30 percent of them actually ended up decreasing employee performance.[46] Another study reported that two-thirds of those receiving the highest ratings in their performance reviews were not the highest-performing employees! With the average number of employees reporting to managers rising from 6 before the 1960s to between 15 and 25 today, keeping tabs on individual performance through dimly remembered anecdotes dating back six or even twelve months has become daunting at best and highly inaccurate and dispiriting at worst.

In 2011, Kelly Services was one of the first major professional services firms to drop appraisals. PwC followed in 2013 and Deloitte in 2015, and Accenture and KPMG made similar announcements shortly thereafter. Juniper Systems, Dell, Microsoft, Motorola, Netflix, and Cargill were among other early companies to embrace this trend.

---

45 2017 Deloitte Global Human Capital Trends," Deloitte: https://www2.deloitte.com/us/en/pages/human-capital/articles/introduction-human-capital-trends.html

46 "Why Performance Appraisals Don't Improve Performance," Ray Williams, *Psychology Today*: https://raywilliams.ca/why-performance-reviews-dont-improve-performance/

Another company to abandon appraisals was Adobe, who had been studying the possibility of abandoning the dreaded performance review process before finally doing so in 2011, turning instead to what they call an "agile method," which chunks projects into "sprints," followed immediately by check-ins and debriefing sessions. Since introducing this approach, voluntary employee turnover has been reduced by 30 percent.

Patty McCord, former Chief Talent Officer of Netflix, puts it this way, "We held formal reviews for a while, but came to realize they didn't make sense. So we asked managers and employees to have conversations about performance as an organic part of their work. Building a bureaucracy and elaborate rituals around measuring performance usually does not improve it."[47]

THE VALUES-CENTERED LEADERSHIP® MODEL

If performance management systems are generally so ineffective, what should we do in their place? Let's look at another approach.

One way of looking at leadership is to appreciate that high performance anywhere—in our personal or

---

47 "How Netflix Reinvented HR," Patty McCord, *Harvard Business Review*: https://hbr.org/2014/01/how-netflix-reinvented-hr

professional lives—is achieved when we do these three things exceptionally well:

1. Attain great levels of competence (**Mastery**),
2. Build deep, inspiring, and enduring relationships (**Chemistry**), and
3. Serve others (**Delivery**).

Almost any activity in which we engage can be classified under one or more of these three headings. Try thinking of something that you do in your personal or professional life that is not comfortably contained within the rubric of Mastery, Chemistry, or Delivery. These three are called the Primary Values.

We define each of these Primary Values as follows:

1. **Mastery:** Undertaking whatever you do to the highest standards of which you are capable
2. **Chemistry:** Relating so well with others that they actively seek to associate themselves with you
3. **Delivery:** Identifying the needs of others, and meeting them

We achieve these three Primary Values through, respectively:

1. **Learning:** Seeking and practicing knowledge and wisdom
2. **Empathizing:** Considering the thoughts, feelings, and perspectives of others, and
3. **Listening:** Hearing and understanding the communications of others

These last three are called "Accelerators" because they accelerate the Primary Value to which they are linked. For example, greater Learning leads to greater Mastery. We call this combination Values-centered Leadership®.[48]

Achieving Mastery, Chemistry, or Delivery cannot be achieved by wishful thinking alone. There are concrete actions and steps that we can each take that, when purposely applied, will lead to the enhancement and growth of these three Primary Values. In order to achieve greater Mastery, we must engage in new Learning. Similarly, if we wish to build greater Chemistry with people, we must first Empathize with them. And meeting the needs of others—Delivery—is best achieved by Listening for those needs.

These six little words are incredibly powerful because they propel all human progress, innovation, relationships, and achievements. There is nothing in the world that we cannot do if we *learn* something new that leads to greater *Mastery*, *empathize* with others that leads to greater *Chemistry*, or *listen* to the needs of others in order to achieve greater *Delivery*.

The intention here is to replace semiannual or annual performance reviews with frequent, inspiring conversations—check-ins. Let's look at an example: Suppose you pass the desk of one of your employees and

---

48 See the "Torch" section in *The Spark, the Flame, and the Torch: Inspire Self. Inspire Others. Inspire the World*, page 183, The Secretan Center Inc., 2010, ISBN-13: 978-0986565403. See also the Secretan Center Vector 360° Leadership Survey: http://www.secretan.com/tools/assessment-tools/vector-360-leadership-survey/

stop to ask them how they're doing. They tell you that they are wrestling with a challenging customer and they are having a difficult time catching up on backorders. So you ask them, "Where do you feel we are stuck? Is it Mastery (we are just not good enough at what we do)? Or is it Chemistry (we don't have very good personal relationships with this customer)? Or is it Delivery (we are not meeting the customer's needs)?"

Your employee says, "Our Mastery is terrific—we are great at what we do. Our Chemistry is excellent too— we have wonderful relationships with this customer. It just seems that we have difficulty meeting the customer's needs—Delivery." Notice here that you have eliminated two possibilities (Mastery and Chemistry), thereby enabling you to focus on the sole remaining one.

So you might respond with, "Well, the Accelerator for Delivery is Listening. So who do we need to listen to? How do we listen more effectively? What are we not hearing? If the customer were to be completely frank with us, what do you think they would say to us?" And thus begins an authentic, productive, inspiring, and growth-orientated conversation. You might have one of these check-ins every day with every one of your employees, and thus, you become their coach, mentor, feedback expert, inspirer, and friend. And the need for an "annual review" becomes moot.

THE VECTOR

It is possible, but not necessary, to assign numerical values to these questions. For example, you might ask, "How do you feel about your Mastery today?" You might get an answer such as, "It feels like around a 7 for me today." You might respond, "What about your Learning?" and the response might be, "It really feels like a 6 today." Hidden in these responses is a magic formula we call "the Vector," which the dictionary defines as "a quantity possessing both magnitude and direction." If you subtract the Primary Value (in this case Mastery at 7) from the Accelerator (in this case Learning at 6), the resulting number is –1. We call this a *negative Vector of 1* (Figure 5). It suggests that there is insufficient learning occurring at the present time to achieve the appropriate level of Mastery—a 6 in Learning is not sufficient to sustain a 7 in Mastery. One could go further: the current level of Mastery cannot be sustained by this lesser level of Learning because it will lead to an ultimate decline in Mastery. In your role as leader and coach, this guides you into a valuable conversation: "What do you think you need to learn in order to achieve greater Mastery?" Notice that this is a nonjudgmental, noncritical, peer-to-peer conversation designed to inform both parties and enable them both to grow—based on questions, not judgments or lectures.

.

Primary Value	Score (A) 0–10	Accelerators	Score (B) 0–10	Difference (B) – (A)
MASTERY *Undertaking whatever you do to the highest standards of which you are capable*	7	**LEARNING** *Seeking and practicing knowledge and wisdom*	6	–1

FIGURE 5: The Values-centered Leadership® Vector

The Vector is a forward indicator. Most performance appraisals are snapshots of history, looking back over six or 12 months (backward indicator). On the other hand, the Vector takes account of the current situation (a Mastery level of 7 in the above example), recognizing that the current situation is simply the result of the past, and, at the same time, acknowledges that we are equally interested in the future. Furthermore, in the example above, the negative Vector of 1 predicts a future where there are insufficient levels of Learning to propel current levels of Mastery. Since the Vector is negative, it is also signaling a future decline of Mastery. This can result in a rich opportunity for deep and constructive conversation— an inspiring check-in. Since both parties are familiar with the methodology, there is no need to explain it all; there is a natural rhythm to the conversation—a comfortable check-in, which both understand to be completely constructive and forward-looking. An early adopter of the commitment to abandoning performance reviews was Cargill, who have found that there has been a measurable improvement after managers began providing inspiring and constructive feedback that was *forward looking*, instead of reviewing what had happened in the past—a common, and irrelevant, aspect of most performance reviews.

THE PORTABILITY OF VALUES-CENTERED LEADERSHIP®

Another benefit of this methodology is that it can be transferred to almost any activity. A strategic plan, for example, can consist of the three Primary Values and the three matching Accelerators:

1. **Mastery:** What do we need to be really good at to achieve this strategic plan? What will we need to Learn to achieve the level of Mastery required?

2. **Chemistry:** Who are the people who will be instrumental in the successful achievement of this strategic plan? How will we Empathize with those people?

3. **Delivery:** Who are the customers for the strategic plan? What do they need? How will we Listen effectively to them to accurately hear their needs?

Once people understand the generic definitions of Mastery, Chemistry, and Delivery; and Learning, Empathizing, and Listening, they can apply them anywhere—at home or at work.

Customer service check-ins can be handled in the same way—we can ask the customer:

- **Mastery:** How well do you think we do what we do? What do you think we need to **Learn** in order to improve our **Mastery?**

- **Chemistry:** How good are our relationships and how, and with whom, can we relate better? How, and with whom, should we **Empathize** more?

- **Delivery:** Are we meeting your needs? How can we **Listen** better and more, in order to continually improve the way we meet your needs?

The answer to each of these questions, and the mathematical relationship between the Primary Value and the Accelerator with which it is coupled, will yield a *vector*.

Values-centered Leadership® is a very effective coaching tool, and almost all conversations between leaders and their employees and between coaches and their clients are coaching conversations. Perhaps you are coaching a client or an employee who is looking for career guidance. You might ask, "What is your career objective?" The client or employee will define their objective, and this will open the door for the coach to ask a number of questions, all of which are designed to help the employee or client grow and think through for themselves the answers to the big (and small) questions in their lives. For example:

> Mastery: What level of **Mastery** will you need to achieve this career objective? What do you need to **Learn** in order to achieve that level of **Mastery**? From whom will you choose to learn? How can I support you in doing this?
>
> Chemistry: With whom do you need to build stronger relationships—greater **Chemistry**—in order to achieve this career objective? How will you **Empathize** with them? How can I help you in your efforts?
>
> Delivery: Who is the customer; whom will you be serving if you achieve your career objective? What are their needs, and how will you **Listen** effectively to understand those needs well? What help or support can I offer you as you do this?

These examples show that this can be a framework for coaching that can be adapted to the needs of the person being coached under almost any circumstances.

A job description can be structured using the Values-centered Leadership® model. **Mastery:** What are the skills at which I need to excel in this job? **Learning:** What do I need to learn in order to polish and grow those skills? **Chemistry:** With whom must I connect and relate and build inspiring relationships? **Empathy:** How will I empathize with those people and feel the experience of "walking in their moccasins"? **Delivery:** Who is the customer for my job, and what do they need from me? **Listening:** How and to whom shall I listen in order to clearly identify my customer's needs?

One can even apply this methodology in marriage counseling. When couples are trying to repair their relationships, one might ask, "What is not working right now? Is it **Mastery**—he/she is incompetent and a poor provider? Or is it **Chemistry**—I don't love or like him/her anymore? Or is it **Delivery**—he/she doesn't meet my needs?

As you can see, this is a *lingua franca* with the great advantage that once the language is learned (and this can be started with inspiring check-ins that replace performance reviews), it can be easily applied to almost any situation.

MOVING FORWARD WITH AN INSPIRING, CONSTRUCTIVE CHECK-IN INSTEAD OF A PERFORMANCE APPRAISAL SYSTEM

Here are some general tips for reinventing this entire process:

1. **Announce a Clear New Direction:** Declare your intention to introduce an entirely new approach to inspiring people that will become a system-

wide commitment to inspiration. Starbucks did this when Howard Schultz returned as the CEO after the 2008 recession to reinvent the future of the company.

2. **Abolish the Entire Existing System:** Don't tweak. As we have seen, the accountability system of performance appraisals or measurement is broken and therefore beyond repair or tweaking. An entirely fresh approach, starting from scratch, is required, and doing so, in a collaborative design partnership with employees, will energize them and the company, ensure their buy-in, and inspire them.

3. **Create a Conversation among Peers.** One of the many reasons people abhor the traditional performance appraisal process is that it is too often autocratic, top-down, subjective, superficial, critical, judgmental, demeaning, intimidating, and painful. So let's build something that aspires to be the opposite: caring, other-centered, and focused on personal growth and development, in tune with personal aspirations as well as corporate objectives—a process I like to call "attunement." In other words, make it a mutual dialogue of shared interests, which seeks to heal and mend and grow relationships, create possibilities, and inspire both parties—attuning personal and

corporate needs together. The key question to
ask is, "How may I serve you?"

4. **Remove Fear:** Make it clear that the purpose of
the check-in is not to punish, appraise, evaluate,
judge, set compensation, or assess promotional
prospects. There will be no recriminations
or repercussions from the conversation. The
intention is to not record check-ins or store
conversations somewhere in a file in the HR
department. The sole purpose of the check-in is
to seek understanding and to clarify aspirations,
hopes, and dreams and to create a plan to
collaborate in a way that realizes them. Make
it safe to tell the truth—in both directions—
something that rarely happens in traditional
performance appraisals.

5. **Remove Metrics:** Believing that there is any
science in the analytics we typically undertake
is absurd. Leading and inspiring people is an
art—and it can be taught. Focus only on metrics
that are agreed by each party and use only
those metrics to assess progress in the check-ins.
This means that all check-ins are personal and
individual and custom-designed to fit the needs
of each person. The most useful metric is the
Vector, and even then, it should be used only as
an aid in building a growth-oriented, inspiring
contribution or solution to challenges, queries,
and aspirations.

6. **Timing:** Eliminate anything "annual" and replace it with frequent (as in daily) check-ins. Inspiring check-ins, not just about challenges or projects, but about dreams, possibilities, goals, and growth, should be frequent, and part of the ongoing relationship between leaders and their employees. We should particularly emphasize personal dreams—our role as coaches and leaders is to help those we guide to achieve their personal dreams too, not just the corporate objectives. Learning and developmental conversations should occur when projects are completed, goals or milestones achieved, crises or challenges occur, and whenever there are changes to the rhythm of work, the environment, a customer connection or sale, new initiatives, etc. This removes the fear and dread of anticipation that comes from "annual" inquisitions.

7. **Train, Coach, and Partner:** If I were CEO of a major enterprise again, one of the changes I would make would be to replace the word "leader" with "coach," or even "partner." I define coaching as *Inspiring others to grow from where they are to where they aspire to be, seeing through where a person is, to where they **can** be.* Our key role as leaders is to partner with others and coach them. Leaders will need to be educated in a system-wide review of the new

process. Central to this training and coaching will be a raised level of respect for one another and a commitment to be inspiring in the process. It can be useful to ask those we guide these four questions:

a. What am I doing that I should stop?

b. What am I doing that I should do more of because it is working well?

c. What am I *not* doing that I should start doing?

d. What else would I like to try?

8. **Automate:** Capturing frequent conversations and check-ins in today's fast-paced environment can be a hit-and-miss affair unless there are systems available to capture them. A mobile app is an excellent way to do this as it enables leaders to provide feedback anytime and to record it if desired. Of course, technology is useful, but it must be seamlessly integrated with a comforting conversation through a one-to-one connection that draws from and connects to the heart. The best apps require little effort to input, are simple and easy to use, and their sole purpose is to support those using them. General Electric's approach is called the PD@GE app ("PD" stands for "performance development"), which can retrieve notes and documents from prior check-ins and provide summaries. Employees use the same app to ask

for management support when they need it. Amazon has an app too, as does IBM, and in the latter's case, it incorporates the ability to provide feedback to co-workers and offers managers an opportunity to choose whether to send a copy to the recipient's manager or not. Automating check-in conversations offers tracking so that leaders can review previous discussions when considering projects, issues, or new assignments.

One of the finest ways by which we as leaders help to change the world and make it a better place is by coaching, teaching, mentoring, leading, partnering with and inspiring others, helping them to grow and live to their full potential. Almost everyone nurses aspirations to grow, to be more, to make a difference, and to be relevant—in other words, to achieve greater Mastery, Chemistry, and Delivery. Our role as leaders is to help others unlock those possibilities so they can fully live their dreams—not as Henry David Thoreau wrote, in "lives of quiet desperation"—but, as John Quincy Adams noted, in encouraging leaders to help others realize their dreams: "If your actions inspire others to dream more, learn more, do more and become more, you are a leader."

SEVEN

From Salary Grades to Added-Value Compensation

Has anyone ever said to you, "That's above my pay grade!" meaning, "I do not have the authority, I will need to get permission from a person more senior than me in order to give you a decision"? Or perhaps it might mean, "I am stuck at a level in this organization that does not permit me to use my full creative and intellectual powers."

Welcome to the world of pay grades, salary scales, bands, levels, or whatever other name you want to give this legacy approach to compensation.

The origins of many of today's management practices, such as autocracy, top-down command and control, hierarchies and bureaucracies, titles, line and staff distinctions, ranking, operations research, PERT, strategic management, and others we have discussed so far—and yes, pay grades—can be traced back to the early work of Frederick Winslow Taylor, Frank and Lillian Gilbreth, Henry R. Towne, and Henry L. Gantt, the latter working for the Army Bureau of Ordinance. In fact, the military eagerly embraced the theories of these early management scientists because they provided tools with which to rank the readiness of personnel for assignment and promotion, and because they fitted seamlessly into the military's authoritarian management style.

There are few greater irritants in modern organizations than salary grades. The subject of pay grades often breeds resentment, a sense of unfairness, a feeling that the whole subject is shrouded in mystery and manipulated by "the system"—and almost everyone feels they deserve more. Attempts to introduce fairness, comparative thresholds, calibration of ranges, and consideration of market trends are frequently criticized, no matter how much good work and research has been undertaken.

We use salary grades because we believe they save organizational time, they value different positions in the organization appropriately, they have the potential to enhance the reputational value of the organization and retain talent. Pay grades are also used to provide anonymity for individuals—a person's pay grade (range) can be revealed without revealing the actual salary. Most of this is illusory and is more than offset by the criticisms described earlier. Besides, in the age of the Internet and glassdoor.com, accessing personal salary data for an individual has become increasingly simple to do.

TRANSPARENCY

The underlying reason why employees are distrustful and unhappy with pay is that they often feel that compensation is shrouded in mystery, arbitrariness, and opaqueness. Research consistently shows that money is not the top satisfier among employees. But we should be careful with this statistic because the same data consistently shows that money also sits solidly amongst the top five employee satisfiers, even if it is not number one.[49] If employees cannot understand how the compensation system works, what they need to do to increase their

49 "Top 5 Employee Motivators," Robert Tanner, *Management is a Journey:*
https://managementisajourney.com/fascinating-numbers-top-5-employee-motivators/

income, and if the goalposts keep changing and the whole thing seems mysterious—it's no wonder they become disenchanted with compensation policy. And when they learn that the average CEO earns 271 times as much as they do, making the equivalent of the average employee's annual income by noon on New Year's day, resentment can breed.[50]

ADDED-VALUE COMPENSATION

There is a relatively straightforward answer to this dilemma: trust employees, assume that they share the organization's objectives, reveal the inner mathematics of the finances, and show them how they can influence and participate in the rewards enjoyed by the entire organization. As mentioned earlier, this is Alibaba's "blue sky" recipe. This is often referred to as "open book management,"[51] in which employees receive all relevant financial information necessary to help them to be more connected to their work and more effective.

---

50 "CEO Pay Remains High Relative to the Pay of Typical Workers and High-wage Earners," Lawrence Mishel and Jessica Schieder, *Economic Policy Institute*: www.epi.org/publication/ceo-pay-remains-high-relative-to-the-pay-of-typical-workers-and-high-wage-earners/

51 Stack, Jack, and Burlingham, Bo, *The Great Game of Business*, Crown Business, July 2013, ISBN-13: 978-0385348331; https://en.wikipedia.org/wiki/Open-book_management

Perhaps we will have to accept that compensation will always be, to a greater or lesser degree, a bone of contention. And in institutions like academia, healthcare, government, and non-profits, the suggestions in this chapter will need to be adapted to fit the specific context of each organization. But we can help employees develop a sense of ownership in any organization and its purpose, as well as the metrics by which we gauge success, by educating them in all of these areas. This will first require a significant change in leadership philosophy and culture. It can be seen that an organization's approach to compensation is a direct reflection of the organization's culture. *In fact, all of the changes suggested in this book will require a cultural transformation.* Committing to sharing the results of everyone's work and their contribution to the organization requires a level of openness, transparency, collaboration and teamwork, and the removal of silos, individual-based incentives, salary bands, and the like. It will also shift the organization's emphasis from product or service to process. At the deepest level—and perhaps this is the most difficult cultural change to achieve—it requires that we end any sense of entitlement, selfishness, or greed.

GAINSHARING

Gainsharing is an organizational system for sharing the benefits of cost reductions, productivity, and quality improvements and distributing part of the proceeds in the form of bonuses. Gainsharing programs, such as the Scanlon Plan, began in the late 1930s, and Rucker Plans first appeared in the early 1940s. They are an excellent way to help employees understand the connection between their own compensation and the results of the organization. While these plans were, and continue to be, a good step forward, they are not usually ambitious enough or transparent or generous enough to cause employees to feel a deep sense of ownership and participation in the business.

ADDED-VALUE
COMPENSATION PLANS

There are two ways in which employees can contribute to the success of an organization:

1. The amount and source of the organization's revenues
2. Reducing costs

Every member of the organization can affect both of these—the top revenue-generating salesperson can lower costs by turning out lights, and the most efficient accounts receivable manager can share their knowledge of customers with salespeople who can turn that intelligence into new sales opportunities. The first step in creating an added-value compensation program is to change the culture so that everyone is aware that these twin opportunities are available to everyone. The cultural shift is from individualism to oneness—from a group of individual, functional specialists to a united, singular team sharing one dream, regardless of functional role, and a feeling of oneness, not separateness.

The next step is to explain the mathematics of the organization. There is no one right way to do this, but my preference has been to conduct "town hall" meetings in every part of the organization to explain how the corporate culture is changing, how the organization is reinventing its approach to participating in the financial rewards of the organization, and presenting the financial data of the organization. My experience has also taught me to engage everyone directly with their own learning styles. Where some individuals may be very comfortable with numbers and ratios, others may prefer graphics, videos, or metaphors. It's important to understand the learning styles of those with whom we are communicating and then adapt the way the information is presented to fit their different styles.

Explaining the internal mathematics should include a full reveal and definition of:

- The amount and source of the organization's revenues

- The gross margin percentage
- The variable costs or cost of goods sold
- The net margin percentage
- The fixed overheads and their components, especially salaries
- The return on capital required by the organization
- The return expected by shareholders
- The net operating profit expected by the organization
- The anticipated taxes, depreciation, and finance costs

So the presentation to employees, based on the organization's achieving $100,000 of revenues in the period, might look something like this, for example:

	%	$
Revenues	100	$100,000
Gross Margin	60	$60,000
Variable Overhead/Cost of Goods	20	$20,000
Net Margin	40	$40,000
Fixed Overhead	20	$20,000
Net Margin After Fixed and Variable Overhead	20	$20,000
Return on Capital/Finance Costs	3	$3,000
Taxes	3	$3,000
Return on Shareholders' Equity	3	$3,000
Net Profit	11	$11,000

Base salaries should be set in the first or second quartile. The reason for this is that the corporate culture is shifting from a hierarchical or bureaucratic style to an entrepreneurial one. By paying a fair wage that does not seek to be at the top of the market, the company shifts a little of the risk from the organization to the employee. If the company doesn't do well, the employee will share in the poor fortunes while still receiving a fair level of compensation. Conversely, if the company does well, employees will be able to participate in its good fortune. The trade-off for the employee is to give up a little bit of security in exchange for some notional equity in the organization and a significant increase in intrinsic rewards.

Here's how it works: In the example above, the organization has sales of $100,000 and expects to achieve a net margin, after fixed and variable overheads, of 20 percent of revenues ($20,000). A formula is devised in which net margins greater than 20 percent ($20,000) are shared between the company and its employees— let's say in this case 70 percent for the company and 30 percent for the employees. If the net margin comes in at 20 percent or less, there will be nothing to share with employees. If the net margin for a given period comes in at 25 percent above the standard ($25,000), the 5 percent by which the base level has been exceeded represents a 25-percent surplus ($5,000), and this surplus is then shared in the ratio of 70 percent to the organization ($3,500) and 30 percent to the employees ($1,500).

A formula is then devised to share the 30 percent distribution ($1,500) in direct proportion to the salary of each employee in relation to the total salary bill.

This information is transparently shared with all employees each quarter. If the results prove negative or neutral, the information is transparently shared in detail, showing where targets were missed, where improvements could be made, and employee input and suggestions are invited and welcomed. If the results prove to be positive, this presents an opportunity to share successes across departments or divisions and create other learning opportunities. In either case, these meetings provide an opportunity to celebrate the participation, collaboration, contribution, teamwork, and organizational performance of everyone—a key path to achieving a sense of corporate oneness. As a minimum, results should be shared quarterly—and with every employee. Employees will experience a greater sense of control in the organization and a level of "ownership" without being required to invest capital.

This is not the appropriate place to go into the design detail of an added-value compensation program, and in any case, there is no magic recipe for designing the right approach. It's more about the philosophical approach to people and leadership than it is about the mechanics of the added-value program. Moving to an added-value compensation approach is a cultural and leadership shift more than a financial or compensation decision, and one that should be consciously chosen. Once that decision is made, it is followed by deep and wide employee and management participation from all areas of the organization (not just human resources), who co-create the design and implementation details of the program. It will be a constant work in progress with many (perhaps endless) tweaks and iterations as it is frequently adjusted to meet the needs of the organization and its team members, as well as the changing environment and market conditions. Keeping enthusiasm high and employee involvement active, ensuring that everyone contributes to the creation, application, communication, and implementation of the plan, and providing transparent and frequent feedback will cultivate a blossoming sense of "ownership" of the process and lead to a reenergized and more inspiring corporate culture.

Patty McCord, former Chief Talent Officer at Netflix, offers this advice:

> "Here's a simple test: If your company has a performance bonus plan, go up to a random employee and ask, 'Do you know specifically what you should be doing right now to increase your bonus?' If he or she can't answer, the HR team isn't making things as clear as they need to be."[52]

---

52 "How Netflix Reinvented HR," Patty McCord, *Harvard Business Review*: https://hbr.org/2014/01/how-netflix-reinvented-hr

The great quality guru Edwards Deming was once asked if there was a best time to implement a Total Quality Management system. Deming is said to have replied, "It doesn't matter when you start, as long as you begin right away." The same thing applies to an added-value compensation plan.

EIGHT

From Mission Statements to One Dream

Leadership is about inspiring people, and people—every one of us—are inspired by dreams. We are inspired by the dreams of transformational movements; the disadvantaged who dream of, and achieve, greatness; great democracies; cities and states; our families; our marriages; liminal art; and masterful sports—and, of course, great organizations.

A dream is the unique characteristic shared by people and successful teams who undertake great endeavors and attain extraordinary achievements, whether they start revolutions, overthrow despots, found nations, create a new movement, climb mountains, launch startups, reinvent organizations, make breakthroughs, or change the world of ideas, beliefs, knowledge, or discoveries. Each of these is powered by the passion of a dream. Walt Disney said, "If you dream it, you can do it. Always remember that this whole thing was started by a mouse."

Over the last 50 years in corporate life, we have expanded our capacity to quantify, measure, and analyze, but we have stifled our capacity to dream. An old cliché in business goes, "If you don't measure it, it won't get done." But there are so many things that can't be measured, like a symphony or a sonnet, great art or theater, inspiring landscapes, a nurturing friendship, a heartbreak, falling in love or making love (it is strongly advised not to use a spreadsheet to measure the metrics or quality of love-making!). There are many business experiences that are similarly difficult to measure—on the negative side: fear and intimidation, lack of authority, feelings of impotence, being lost in a bureaucracy, the emotional impact of receiving a poor performance review, stress, and overwork;[53] and on the positive side: pride in the company we work for, emotional connection to colleagues and customers, commitment to the team, love for a leader, the joy derived from a job well done,

---

53 The free Secretan Center Inc. Job Burnout Survey will provide an indication of your stress levels at work - www.secretan.com/tools/assessment-tools/ job-burnout-survey/

meaning and fulfillment at work, making a difference or a contribution to the world, nourishment of the soul at work.[54]

For a long time, we have known that having a dream is an integral part of greatness—in sports, in politics, in business, in religion—in life. Yet we are still hooked on the mundane language of "mission, vision, and values." We repeatedly take the tired old way, because it is a classic example of the Bellwether Effect—it is familiar and "everyone does it," and so we conform. And the futility of mission statements creates dissonance. The conventional wisdom in business is that dreaming is too "out there," so we seldom talk about it in an organizational context. Instead, we fall back on the traditional mission, vision, and values statements, and yet, these seem so stale and barren when compared to the inspiring power of a dream.

Many people have subjective views about what an ambitious corporate aspiration should look like. But it is dangerous to make such momentous decisions on the basis of "hunches," prejudices, biases, or majority votes. Many leadership decisions—across sectors and issues—are largely made by intuition, or "gut instinct." They are, in the end, intelligently derived "best guesses." Leaders often then use tools such as traditional market research and the opinions of those around them to

---

54 The free Secretan Center Inc. Soulscreen Test will measure how much your work nourishes your soul — www.secretan.com/tools/assessment-tools/soulscreen/

validate their best guesses, even though these methods are often demonstrably flawed.

The cartoonist Scott Adams once created a three-column word selector to enable the unimaginative—"The Boss" in the Dilbert cartoon strip for example—to create a mission statement. The intent, I think, was to poke fun at the banality of mission statements.

Proclaiming that you wish to be the "best, most customer-focused and successful company in the widget business in the nation" will cause eyes to roll and smartphones to be activated to relieve the boredom. One of the weaknesses about mission statements is that they are so often about *me*. Disappointing though this may be for some leaders to hear, customers and employees are not always interested in *you*—they are far more interested in knowing how you will serve, make a difference, and make the world a better place—not how you are going to become bigger and richer and increase shareholders' wealth. A mission statement may be about *you*, but a dream is about *others* and how you will serve them.

In some of my keynote speeches, I ask the audience if they have a mission statement. Almost everyone does. Then I tell them that if I were to collect all of their mission statements, shuffle them, and return them in random order, most wouldn't know if they got their own mission statement back or not! I've even tried this by taking the mission statements of three of the largest healthcare organizations in the country, returning them in the wrong order, and then asking them which one is theirs—and they couldn't tell—they just guessed! How can we achieve our mission if we can't remember it?

We are in a new era in which people want something more inspiring than a mission statement—something that gathers the energy of an organization into a compelling, exciting, and energizing description of a future desired state, and this does not fit easily under the heading of "mission, vision, and values." A much larger container is needed to hold a magnificent idea. We need a dream, a new way of positioning businesses, teams, cities, communities, countries—and individuals, so that they can become reinvigorated, inspired, and passionate again.

How did we land a man on the moon? U.S. President John F. Kennedy had a dream that millions embraced, making it their own and making it real. Indeed, the dream was so powerful that it restored America's self-esteem, which had been deflated after the Russians launched Sputnik. This dream galvanized the nation and inspired much of the rest of the world. Dreams are like that. They transcend differences, disagreements, and petty arguments and engage us in a higher purpose, uniting us as *one*. It is this elusive oneness for which we all yearn, because when we feel a sense of oneness—belonging to something larger than ourselves—we become inspired. A dream has a unique capacity to achieve oneness because everyone can align behind a single shared purpose—*one* team focused on *one* dream.

Great historical leaders—Christ, Buddha, Lao-Tzu, Confucius, Mohammed, Nelson Mandela, Mother Teresa, Abraham Lincoln, and Martin Luther King, Jr., among them—all knew how impactful a dream can be. In his famous 1963 speech on the steps of the Lincoln Memorial in Washington, DC, King repeated the phrase "I have a dream" eight times. His ability to articulate this dream united and inspired hundreds of thousands of people, who sensed a feeling of unmet oneness, and ushered in a new era in civil rights.

That is the power of dreams—the power to change the world.

To understand how modern leadership can transform organizations, communities, countries, and the world, we must understand and harness the power of the dream.

A dream is a whole order of magnitude greater than a mission statement. We are not talking about a two-percent increase in market share or five-percent improvement in employee satisfaction—but a bold, daring, impudent, audacious, outrageous, thrilling, exhilarating—and deeply inspiring *dream*.

What is so interesting about a bold dream such as "landing a man on the moon," or an ambitious corporate aspiration is that it has three remarkable features:

1. At the time the dream is created, no one has a clue how it will be achieved because it is of a higher order than anything that the organization has done so far, and therefore it will be

necessary to discover and implement entirely new ideas and approaches to achieve the dream. Intense mutual collaboration results.

2. Achieving the dream will change everything. It will require different resources, people, training, organizational design, marketing, technology, infrastructure, knowledge and skills, research, and much more, and this will change the very nature—and the culture—of the organization. One of our clients spent $4 billion on acquisitions, following the creation of their dream statement, to fill in the gaps in their portfolio that would have prevented them from realizing their dream.

3. For the first time, everyone will have a shared higher purpose—a sense of oneness—and the entire organization will be dedicated to achieving it. Whatever the activity in the organization, it will have to successfully pass this test: "Is this helping us to achieve our dream?"

THE TRUTH BELOW
THE CONSCIOUS MIND

Every organization, city, state, province, or country yearns to be distinctive and great. To achieve this, they typically commission consultants to conduct conventional research from which is developed a strategy that, in turn, often leads to an implementation and change management program. The success rate of this sequence is shockingly low. Ninety-five percent of new products fail.[55] Pollsters frequently fail to identify outcomes.[56] Mergers frequently fail or come unglued.[57] Dreams are often dashed.[58]

The reason for these failures is that there are always "subjective" inputs in conventional research—ego and "turf" interests, the "mood" being personally experienced by the survey subject, baggage, and agendas—all of which will inevitably leach into, and pollute, the data gathered. Conventional research methodology collects and assesses data that is infused with subjective input from respondents because it is obtained from the conscious mind. Asking questions like, "What business should we be in?" or "What do you think our Mission should be?" or "How can we improve our services?" will always draw from the conscious mind of the respondent, complete with all its biases and opinions. This makes it very difficult to access "the truth."

55 "Clay Christensen's Milkshake Marketing," Carmen Nobel, *Working Knowledge*, Harvard Business School: https://hbswk.hbs.edu/item/clay-christensens-milkshake-marketing

56 "What's the Matter With Polling?," Cliff Zukin, *New York Times*: https://www.nytimes.com/2015/06/21/opinion/sunday/whats-the-matter-with-polling.html

57 "83% Of Mergers Fail—Leverage A 100-Day Action Plan For Success" George Bradt, *Forbes*: https://www.forbes.com/sites/georgebradt/2015/01/27/83-mergers-fail-leverage-a-100-day-value-acceleration-plan-for-success-instead/#7c94eade5b86

58 "10 of the most-funded startups to fail in 2017, Matt Burns, *Techcrunch.com*: https://techcrunch.com/gallery/10-of-the-most-funded-startups-to-fail-in-2017/

The Structural Mapping Process® (SMP) is a unique process that bypasses the filters of the conscious mind and therefore reveals insights from a deeper level of awareness. The SMP process was developed by a world-renowned statistician as a solution to the issues raised by Kenneth Arrow, who was awarded the Nobel Prize in 1972 for discovering what was later named "Arrow's Paradox"—the mathematical proof that aggregating individual preferences (i.e., traditional polling, market, and employee surveys and focus groups) cannot lead to an accurate assessment of collective preference.

In a project we undertook recently for a big-city Chamber of Commerce, the director told me that his organization was made up of many interest groups—big business, small business, taxpayers, women's groups, indigenous people, healthcare providers, unions, minority groups, government, academia, and more. His challenge was to get them all to agree on one direction for his organization. But when he conducted conventional research, he found that the responses received were all different. For example, big business responded that they wanted opportunities to grow, lower taxes, increased trade, and expanded profits, and unions responded that they wanted better wages, improved healthcare and safety, and a larger role in decision-making—almost opposite aspirations and agendas. This was true for many of the groups. He just couldn't find a way to arrive at a unified strategic direction. And when he tried, he found the only way to reach agreement was to downgrade ambitions to the lowest common denominator, where there was universal agreement and homogeneity, and this resulted in mediocrity. The traditional approach to corporate transformation, strategy, and visioning initiatives frequently involves conventional research and committee deliberations and negotiating trade-offs because managers feel it is important to incorporate all of the opinions and needs of internal parties so they are represented in the final outcome, what I have heard referred to as "collective ownership of the outcome." But this often results in "vanilla" approaches that feel as if they came out of the same consultant-cookie-kitchen because they tend to be massaged endlessly until an acceptable consensus is achieved. A dream lifts the conversation above the day-to-day agendas so that a dialogue can take place at a higher level and true alignment can happen more naturally.

THE MEME

Any corporate culture operates on the basis of a specific but often invisible "belief structure," composed of paths and key nodes, much like the neural structure of the brain. This belief structure accounts for why some ideas, strategies, brands, and products experience unexpected success—and others fail to gain traction, despite immense HR, operational, or marketing investments. If there is a repeating cycle of ideas—or what we call a "meme"— then there is "permission" for the idea. A meme is a self-replicating and self-perpetuating sequence of ideas.[59] Solutions for how to realize an organizational dream, retain employees, and achieve exceptional customer satisfaction stem directly from revealing and analyzing the belief structure and uncovering the memes that exist about an organization among core constituents, stakeholders, and communities.

PERMISSION SPACE

This, in turn, reveals what I refer to as "permission space." Permission space is defined as "the strength and direction of the energy that will be freely offered by all core constituents to help achieve a dream." I define core constituents as "employees, customers, competitors, unions, media, government, regulators, community and interest groups, politicians, non-profits, industry associations, opinion formers and thought leaders, and any others who, in some way or another, are stakeholders

---

59 A more complete definition of "meme" may be found here: https://en.wikipedia. org/wiki/Meme

and influencers that can shape the future of the organization."

In understanding the concept of the energy of permission space, I have found lessons learned from white-water kayaking to be helpful. "White water" is a fact of life for most of us, and in a business setting, this is often technically referred to as VUCA (volatility, uncertainty, complexity, and ambiguity), a permanent condition that metaphorically resembles white water. To navigate white water, we can 1) attempt the futile— try to fight or overwhelm the energy, or 2) ignore it, discarding the evidence, or 3) we can harness and ride it—flowing and riding with the energy. Riding the energy requires less effort and engages the powerful forces that are moving in the direction in which we wish to travel anyway.

The rule for organizational strategy—indeed for life (because they are one)—is to recognize the direction of the available energy and then ride and harness it. This enables us to become authentic; read the original, core source of power; interpret its direction and momentum; and then use its energetic force to help propel us to our strategic aspiration.

Though an organization may embark on a strategy, say a Lean Six Sigma initiative, and it may be well designed and implemented by the best experts in the world—its success will be limited if it does not "read, recognize, and ride" the white water of the "permission space."

(Of the 54 Fortune 100 companies who have adopted Six Sigma since 1990, the stocks of 91 percent of them have trailed the S&P 500—a failure of leadership, not Six Sigma.) The Bellwether Effect may also explain why, in a multiyear research effort into more than 200 well-established management practices that were deployed over a ten-year period by 160 companies, researchers found that "most of the management tools and techniques we studied had no direct causal relationship to superior business performance."[60] This is because, as described in Chapter 6, initiatives such as performance improvement "programs" are seldom successful on their own—but radical and inspiring changes in leadership approach and employee spirit, and a reinvention of corporate culture, accompanied by state-of-the-art processes are.

A plan to change an organization, internally or externally, is only as good as the insights—and more importantly, *the human passion*—that inform it. Therefore, accurate and better research methodologies need to inform our most important strategies. A dream that is built upon permission space and fueled by extraordinary passion will invariably lead to its success. We cannot achieve bold dreams unless we have first discovered the available permission space. This permission space, when freely available and offered by core constituents,

---

60 "What Really Works," Nitin Nohria, William Joyce, and Bruce Roberson, *Harvard Business Review*: https://hbr.org/2003/07/what-really-works

will power an idea, philosophy, political campaign, product launch, organizational transformation, or a new strategy.

The successful implementation of any strategy—the realization of a dream—depends on its full endorsement by all those whom it will affect. No dream can be achieved unless all of the necessary energy from all of the necessary core constituents is aligned behind it.

In collaboration with my colleagues Wahn Yoon and Penelope Fridman, the founders of L'Institut Idée, and using their proprietary research methodology called the Structural Mapping Process®, we have developed a breakthrough system that identifies the *real* passions of constituents in relation to a proposed decision or aspirational strategy. The system "reads" the energy of the white water of an organization's core constituents and enables us to harness it and ride it—identifying what permission space exists among the core constituents or key stakeholders and uncovering the path that will inspire the greatest passion. Unlike conventional processes, this approach "flies below the radar" of people's subjective opinions, reaching something closer to "the truth" and therefore identifying authentic desires. In another recent case, we worked with the mayor of a large city who told us that he wanted to invite a very powerful and influential local developer to the process in which we would help them define the city's dream, but he was concerned that the larger-than-life developer would influence or manipulate the discussions and the outcome. I explained to him that the process we use is opaque and uninterpretable to a lay person, because it flies below the radar of the conscious mind, and that he would therefore not be able to understand it well enough to manipulate it, and this is how, indeed, it turned out.

THE ONE DREAM® PROCESS

We call the system we use to create an organizational dream the "One Dream® process." We chose this name because it's very important for any organization to have *only one* dream, no matter how large it is. Multiple dreams—or even mission statements—are confusing and dissipate energy. The core philosophy behind the One Dream® process is to find a true understanding of "human aspirations"—a key imperative in developing a meaningful and effective blueprint for change. The process is designed to uncover:

- A deep and certain understanding of the needs of an organization, the marketplace, and the community
- A deep and certain understanding of the core essence of an organization, marketplace, or community

- The activities, lines of business, or strategies that should be discontinued because there is no "permission space" for them
- What can be leveraged to achieve a desired outcome, or dream
- A plan for how the organization will need to adapt in order to realize and then sustain the dream
- Successful and sustainable implementation

The unique advantage of the Structural Mapping Process® is that it reveals the permission space through its ability to bypass the filters that often lead to false or skewed answers. Then, leveraging the permission space, with its brilliantly revealed clarity, one can build on this foundation and harness the organization's subsequent energy and passion to identify and then realize the One Dream®.

CREATING THE ONE DREAM®

There are three steps to creating a dream:
1. Identifying the dream
2. Realizing the dream
3. Sustaining the dream

Over decades of working with organizations, I've discovered two things about corporate dreams: firstly, for a dream to be successful, organizations should expect that their capacity, energy, and resources will be allocated this way: 10 percent for identifying the dream, 20 percent for realizing the dream, and 70 percent for sustaining the dream. Where most organizations become challenged is in maintaining the energy behind the dream over the long haul. The longest that I have seen the dream sustained was 12 years. This was in a global office furniture manufacturer who lost their confidence in their dream when the 2008 recession arrived and their sales of office furniture fell off a cliff. As a consequence, they panicked, reverting to the traditional fear-based, motivational leadership practices (which had become ingrained during the era of their previous leadership style) in the vain hope that it would lead to a rapid turnaround in their fortunes. It didn't work. Starbucks temporarily lost their dream too, resulting in the return of Howard Schultz to the company as its CEO with the express purpose of reinvigorating their original dream, which is "to create the third place."

We arrive at ONE Dream® by

- creating the permission space map
- identifying the dream
- clarifying all of the functional actions and moving parts that the organization must change, accelerate, or terminate in order to realize the ONE Dream®
- creating a summary of every necessary action to realize the ONE Dream® Plan

- creating a digital dashboard that monitors progress, in real time, on all of the necessary actions steps that are contained in the ONE Dream® Plan, thus enabling leaders to monitor daily progress toward the ONE Dream®
- celebrating the milestones as they are achieved

The central philosophy that powers the ONE Dream® process is the belief in dreams to inspire organizations and communities and their stakeholders to outstanding performance. Modern organizations have forgotten how to dream and instead have adopted stale and dry mission, vision, and values statements. Mission statements often fail to arouse passion, but dreams (and the expectation that they can be realized) always arouse passion.

Ultimately, the dream becomes part of the organization's DNA. It is the reason we exist and is so deeply woven into our behavior, culture, and belief system that we don't need to keep reminding ourselves of it—we just live it. When Gandhi was asked to define his mission, he replied, "I don't have a mission—my life is my mission." Mission statements are usually created by committees who strive to please all participants and impress the world, but no great pioneer in history would have settled for the mediocrity of most mission statements.

All great organizations have dreams—think Starbucks, Southwest Airlines, Patagonia, Apple, Alibaba, Google, Facebook, and Amazon—all founded on a dream. Also founded on a dream are Louisville, Kentucky and Austin, Texas. If an organization aligns its entire cultural architecture and energy behind the realization of a dream, breakthrough results—big dreams—can happen for people, customers, the organization, and the community. When everyone aligns behind a dream, quantum changes result!

Leaders among our clients have come up with some remarkable examples of dreams—hospitals who dream of eliminating all avoidable deaths, banks who dream of changing the world, corporations who dream of becoming champions of the environment, communities who dream of becoming world-class centers of excellence and innovation, insurance companies who dream of making the world healthier, cities who dream of becoming the idea capital of the world, and states or provinces who want to be a magnet for the world. It's easy to see how such big aspirations have the power to lift the hearts and minds of everyone involved.

We don't need expensive and convoluted market research and complex theories for this. It's pretty straightforward. When we reveal what's possible, even if never attained before, and identify it as a dream that we hold dear and seek to realize, and then make the commitment to align the entire team or organization behind everything necessary to achieve that dream—the dream becomes possible.

Martin Luther King, Jr., showed us the power of being committed to a dream. So did John F. Kennedy. So can you.

NINE

From War to Peace

Toward the end of World War II, Harry Truman, Winston Churchill, and Joseph Stalin met at Potsdam, where they drafted an ultimatum for the Japanese that they hoped would end the war. Known as the Potsdam Declaration, it called for the Japanese to surrender. The Japanese responded with the word *mokusatsu*, which can be translated in a number of different ways, including "to ignore" or "to withhold comment." (The word is composed of two kanji characters: 黙 [moku "silence"] and 殺 [satsu "killing"]). The Japanese meant to communicate that they wished to withhold comment, so they could confer, and then make a decision. But the Allied Powers were mistakenly informed by inaccurate translators that *mokusatsu* meant that the Japanese were choosing to ignore the Potsdam Declaration.[61] The war was ended shortly afterwards, when the Allies dropped nuclear bombs on Nagasaki and Hiroshima, thus forever transforming the world in which we live.[62] One word resulted in 200,000 deaths. As Pearl Strachan Hurd ironically observed, "Handle them carefully, for words have more power than atom bombs."

Does the story above arouse shock, fear, sadness, or disgust? If so, you are experiencing the power of words to affect your biochemistry and therefore your emotions.

The power of words is perhaps the most important and misunderstood aspect of human communication. Language is rooted in the most primitive parts of our brain. Researchers believe that humans learned to utter sounds only recently—around 100,000 years ago—by mimicking birds, and later, needing to add dimensions to their communications, borrowing additional sounds from primates.[63]

---

61 National Security Agency | Central Security Service: https://www.nsa.gov/ news-features/declassified-documents/tech-journals/assets/files/mokusatsu.pdf

62 "Good Translation Might Have Prevented Hiroshima," Opinion, *New York Times*: www.nytimes.com/1989/08/21/ opinion/l-good-translation-might-have-prevented-hiroshima-322089.html

63 "The Integration Hypothesis of Human Language Evolution and the Nature of Contemporary Languages," Shigeru Miyagawa, Shiro Ojima, Robert C. Berwick and Kazuo Okanoya, *Frontiers in Psychology*: https://www.frontiersin.org/ articles/10.3389/fpsyg.2014.00564/full

In business, we have succumbed to a cliché-ridden tribal language that falls into two categories. The first category consists of buzzword clichés such as meta, outside the box, drill down, granular, ballpark, game-changer, bottom line, thought leader, wheelhouse, organic growth, leverage, Millennial/GenX/GenY, disruptive, best of breed, cutting edge, hit the ground running, big data, pivot, going forward, etc.

The second category is *warrior-speak*, where we use violence-laced metaphors like kill the competition, fight for customers, win the battle, invade markets, fire a salvo, attack opportunities, etc. Mature markets are often described as "battlegrounds," and "victors" are those road "warriors" who are "battle ready" and can "obliterate" or "kill" the competition—the "enemy." We decide a "plan of attack" and then "pull the trigger" or "pull the pin" as we "launch" campaigns. If an initiative "bombs," we declare a "truce." Sometimes we "bombard," or even "carpet bomb," markets, and if we are "attacked," we go into "foxholes." We test strategies by "firing salvoes," which often result in "pitched battles" with competitors and might require us to initiate a "fire storm" in the social media. We lead the "troops from the front" and celebrate "troopers" or "good soldiers."

The buzzword clichés are simply mind numbing, boring, and show that a speaker has a poor grasp of the richness and potential of the English language.

Warrior-speak is more problematic because it myth-
ologizes ruthlessness, and this trips the mind and the
heart and alters our hard-wired emotions. There is a
big difference between business and war—business
has the power to inspire and improve the world and
all its inhabitants—war can never do that. Business
brings opportunities and many blessings; war brings
devastation and destruction.

Whenever we communicate with each other, we
alter our own biochemistry as well as that of those with
whom we are communicating—for better or worse.
Each interaction with another's biochemistry creates
different results in those with whom we communicate—
happiness or sadness, elation or depression, mediocrity
or greatness. We all have immense powers with which
we can heal or wound one another's souls—with every
word we utter. If all the metaphors we use have their
roots in violence and war, we run the risk of creating
paranoia and a lack of sensitivity to ruthlessness,
leading to heightened stress levels in others. And stress,
as researchers have discovered, can lead to long-term
changes in the brain's structure and function, as well as
to mental illness.[64]

Thoughts of war and violence have a profound effect
on our biochemistry, which affects us at a subconscious
level—and, as we shall see, inspiration can be accurately

---

64 "New Evidence that Chronic Stress Predisposes Brain to Mental Illness,"
     Robert Sanders, Media Relations, *UC Berkley News*: http://news.berkley.
     edu/2014/02/11/chronic-stress-predisposes-brain-to-mental-illness/

identified as a biochemical condition in our bodies. Words such as "kill" or "enemy" can create fear, raise stress hormones in our bodies, and cause multiple illnesses. Words such as "joy" and "love" can bring about changes in our genes, strengthen our cognitive abilities, and stimulate resiliency and the emotional centers of the brain. Humans are hardwired to worry— the well-known "fight-or-flight" response—and warrior-speak can set off neurochemicals that can increase the activity of the amygdala (the primitive center of the brain where emotions, including fear, reside), causing the release of stress hormones and neurotransmitters that might be useful if a saber-toothed tiger appeared on your doorstep, but are not very useful—or healthy— in a modern business setting. These neurochemicals, aroused by the emotions triggered by violent language, interrupt or shut down the brain's higher cognitive functions (logic, reason, and language), the very mental processing power that is essential to high performance in business.[65]

The brain is made up of both "gray matter" and "white matter." Gray matter is a major component of the central nervous system, densely packed with nerve cell bodies, and is responsible for the brain's higher functions such as thinking, computing, and decision-making. White matter is comprised of a network of nerve fibers (axons)

65 See, for example, *"Words Can Change Your Brain: 12 Conversation Strategies to Build Trust, Resolve Conflict, and Increase Intimacy,"* by Andrew Newberg, MD and Mark Robert Waldman, Avery, 2012, ISBN-13: 978-1594630903

that interconnect and communicate between brain regions. White matter gets its name from the sheath of white, fatty substance (myelin) that insulates the axons and speeds the flow of electrical signals between neurons and brain regions. Scientists have discovered that chronic stress and the accompanying elevated levels of the steroid hormone cortisol can generate overproduction of myelin-producing cells and underproduction of neurons. We can deduce from this that warrior-speak raises stress levels, which reduces cognitive skills and the executive functions of the brain—making us less effective as leaders, and as humans.

THE BIOCHEMISTRY OF LANGUAGE

Let's look at what happens when we use warrior-speak, violent language, or when we are subjected to abuse by aggressive and hostile individuals. When a stressful situation occurs, such as a statement within which is buried a war metaphor, the body's highly complex and sensitive sensory network transmits information to the cortex, alerting it to danger. Signals are relayed to the amygdala (home of the stress or "fight-or-flight" response), which reacts to them by sending messages to the pituitary gland. Stress hormones are released by the adrenal glands, including cortisol. Elevated cortisol levels interfere with learning and memory, lower immune function and bone density, increase weight gain, blood pressure, cholesterol, heart disease, and interfere with sleep and more. Elevated cortisol levels also increase risk for depression, mental illness, and lower life expectancy and can prompt decreased resilience—especially in adolescence.[66] Medical researchers have noted that depressed patients are unable to maintain appropriate levels of lymphocytes, including T-cells (thymus-affected helper and suppresser cells that fight viral, fungal, and bacterial infection), B-cells (helper cells that are manufactured in the bone marrow), and NK-cells (natural killer cells that spontaneously recognize and kill tumor- and virus-infected cells). This leaves the body more vulnerable to illness and therefore greater depression. Simply put, warrior-speak is toxic and makes us sick. One can notice that employees who are "motivated" by fear take many more paid sick days off than those who are "inspired" by the love for what they do and with whom they do it. One study reported that more than half of absenteeism is caused by stress, which is usually prompted by fear.[67]

---

66 "Chronic Stress Can Damage Brain Structure and Connectivity," Christopher Bergland, *Psychology Today*: https://www.psychologytoday.com/blog/the-athletes-way/201402/chronic-stress-can-damage-brain-structure-and-connectivity

67 "The True Picture of Workplace Absenteeism," Morneau Shepell Research Report: http://www.morneaushepell.com/sites/default/files/documents/3679-true-picture-workplace-absenteeism/9933/absencemanagementreport06-08-15.pdf

CHOOSING OXYTOCIN
VERSUS CORTISOL

If I were to proclaim, "This is chocolate cake to die for," I might intend it as a playful figure of speech—but the word "die" switches on biochemicals that make us sick—even when we do not intend this consequence. If I say, "This is chocolate cake to *live* for!" different biochemicals are released, including oxytocin, the so-called "love hormone," which strengthens our immune system, builds health, and leads to personal inspiration.

Oxytocin is a neurotransmitter and a peptide hormone that is produced in the hypothalamus, then travels to, and is secreted by, the pituitary gland, at the base of the brain. In humans, oxytocin is thought to be released during hugging, a handshake, touching, cuddling a puppy, and orgasm in both genders—and by the use of positive phrasing. It contributes to relaxation, trust, social recognition, empathy, generosity, social memory, bonding, and psychological stability.

WARRIOR-SPEAK

Below I have created a list of simple phrases we use every day, all demonstrating the overuse of warrior-speak in our lives. Can you find a replacement for each of these that would generate oxytocin instead of cortisol and thus boost the immune system instead of suppressing it?

You're killing me	Go to hell	To die for
That was killer	Holy crap	Blow my mind
The bomb	If looks could kill	I'd kill for that
Blow me away	That's sick	Drop-dead gorgeous
Blew it out of the water	Worth a shot (give it a shot)	Let's destroy them
Motivated the hell out of me	That was explosive	That was the bomb
I'm dying	Shoot me now	I hate [....]
Bust a gut	Bulletproof	Oh, shoot!
If I told you I'd have to kill you	That's sick	You slay me
You break me up	You crack me up	Combating issues – i.e., "fighting cancer," "war on drugs"
Love you to death	Magic bullet	Win the battle, but lose the war
Blow it up	Don't beat yourself up!	Dead in the water
Plan of attack	Kill your chances	(chocolate cake) to die for

We have choices. The choice between "kill" or "love" is like the choice between the touch of a tarantula's legs on one's skin and the touch of a lover's hand, because they each set off, respectively, negative or positive electrochemical reactions in the limbic system, the hypothalamus, and therefore throughout the body. Similarly, reprimands, threats, and punishments stimulate negative electrochemical reactions, compared with the positive electrochemical reactions stimulated by encouragement, praise, saying thank you, and behaving with grace.

When we hear warrior-speak or fear-based language, we have choices too. We can be intimidated by the fear or we can rise above it, releasing the appropriate biochemistry necessary to reduce the emotional pain and respond with love. Only the mind can manifest fear. The options chosen determine the biochemical reactions in the limbic system and therefore the quality of work and life.

We can also choose to remove negative words from our daily conversation when they are not absolutely necessary—for example, "Don't do that" is not as effective (and certainly not as inspiring) as "Do you think that's a useful thing to be doing right now?" Words like "no" and "not" can carry deep memories from our childhood, when, for many of us, scolding with negative phrases became embedded in our subconscious. Our self-talk can create the same effect, such as when we say something like, "Boy, I'm an idiot." This wouldn't inspire another, so it will probably not inspire us when we say it to ourselves either. And we can rephrase our communications with a conscious choice to remove negative phrasing and replace it with positive and inspiring phrasing. For example, instead of saying, "No problem" in response to receiving a "thank you" from someone, try, "It was my pleasure" or "You are more than welcome."

As a general guideline, it is always best to ask questions instead of making assertions. For example, "I don't think that is the best strategy" is not as effective (and certainly not as inspiring) as, "Tell me why you think that is the best strategy." The former invites argument and criticism; the latter invites non-threatening and constructive dialogue.

The fans of warrior-speak are sometimes prone to using passive-aggressive language designed to intimidate. For example, one of the many negative words we use in business is "accountable," as in, "I am going to hold you accountable!" We would never use such an intimidating, fear-based term in any other part of our lives except work. Imagine the trouble you would get into if you told your spouse, "I'm going to hold you accountable!" As W. Edwards Deming once proclaimed, "Hold everybody accountable? Ridiculous!"

All human communications are transmitted and received on a continuum ranging between negative and positive, fear and love. Which biochemicals are released by the brain depends on whether a person is experiencing pain and fear, which releases stress hormones, including cortisol; activates the limbic system and puts the body in "stress mode"; or love and pleasure, releasing oxytocin and the "uppers" that lower blood pressure, heart rate, and oxygen consumption. Since the soul and the body are one, whether we are experiencing love or fear directly influences us to the core of our being.

All this suggests that when we use warrior-speak at work or at home, we cause human depression and stress, which compromises the immune system. This creates a dysfunctional environment, both in our bodies and within our organizations. The result is dis-ease and sickness of the soul.

After a meeting with a colleague or friend, you might find yourself wondering, "Why don't I feel good after meeting with that person?" Reflect on the meeting: though the intent, and the person, may have embodied all of the best attributes you most enjoy in others, the overuse of warrior-speak may have had a negative, subconscious, biochemical effect on your emotions. We are drawn to people whose language, communication style, and interaction rely on everything positive. It doesn't mean we must sugarcoat everything, but we can always think of ways to say things in a way that lifts people up rather than putting them down. Warrior-speak and cortisol generation is fear- and motivation-based; positive language is love- and inspiration-based.

If we want to create organizations that are inspiring, it's important for us to understand the power of both the words and the music—what we say *and* how we say it—that we use to communicate internally and externally.

The use of toxic, violent language—whether it is in jest, as a metaphor, or as a literal statement—sets off neurochemicals that release stress hormones and compromise the immune system. And the opposite is also true—if we want to be inspiring, and to inspire others, we need to overhaul our philosophy of language, choose our words carefully, and communicate in peace, not in war. Such a change can transform the culture and reputation of any organization.

As Laurence Olivier spoke in the musical "Time":

"For each life is linked to all life, and your words carry with them chain reactions, like a stone that is thrown into a pond. If your thinking is in order, your words will flow directly from the heart creating ripples of love. If you truly want to change your world, my friends, you must change your thinking. Reason is your greatest tool, it creates an atmosphere of understanding...which leads to caring...which is love. Choose your words with care. Go forth...with love.

Why It Is So Hard to Change

This book is about change. I realize that embracing many of the ideas in its pages will require personal and organizational transformation and culture change— both steep mountains to climb. Resistance to change is both a psychological reaction as well as a physiological one, because change requires the brain to work harder. Our bodies favor homeostasis—the tendency of a system, especially the physiological system of higher animals, to maintain internal stability. The neurobiology of humans is wired to seek homeostasis. Whether you embrace change or not will depend on your approach to new ideas, or ideas that may differ from your own. Sometimes we can mistake new ideas as a criticism of the way we are doing things. But instead of looking at it this way, we can also see it as a new window through which we can view our personal and professional landscapes.

Regardless of what we have covered together in this book, unless there is a commitment to change, your situation will be no different now, or in the future, than it was when you opened the book for the first time— nothing different will happen. If we are to do anything different from what we have been doing, we will need to embrace change. And that will require us to override our natural tendency to seek homeostasis.

A quick scan of the human condition suggests that we need to embrace change in numerous areas—leadership, the environment, politics, healthcare, social justice, and so many more. And yet we are highly resistant to change, even in the face of significant problems or impending disaster. Numerous studies of heart attack patients show that more than one in four will not change their lifestyle to avoid a recurrence, even though they will all hear the same stern lecture every time from the cardiologist who just saved their life.[68]

There are four main reasons why it is so difficult to change.

---

68 "JAMA: Heart Attacks Do Not Always Shock Patients into Shape,"
    Advisory Board: https://www.advisory.com/daily-briefing/2013/04/18/
    jama-heart-attacks-do-not-always-shock-patients-into-shape

1. PARADIGMS

Albert Einstein wrote, "We cannot solve our problems with the same level of thinking that created them." He also said, "Common sense is the collection of prejudices acquired by age eighteen." This takes us to the first reason why we find it so difficult to change—paradigms. What Einstein was referring to is the way each of us becomes locked into "paradigms."

Ever since the publication of Thomas Kuhn's *The Structure of Scientific Revolutions* in 1962, the notion of the paradigm has been a popular concept. Students graduate within the framework of a specific discipline, complete with rules, assumptions, beliefs, and strictly prescribed ways to make decisions. This becomes our operating paradigm—a box—and if we step out of the box, we will not graduate. Once we have internalized what our teachers deem to be *the* operating paradigm, all other paradigms appear as wrong, flawed, or silly. Thus equipped, our new paradigm becomes our intellectual operating software, and we become convinced that ours is the *only* right, sensible, and objective way of doing things. Our paradigm is the very water in which we swim, and to be asked to leave this warm and comfortable environment is not only unthinkable, but perhaps even dangerous. We do not ask questions from inside the box—the box *is* the answer. If the rest of the world is not of our paradigm, the rest of the world is wrong. The box is comfortable—it is what we know—a new paradigm represents the unknown. We see this vividly demonstrated in our politics every day—views that support our own paradigm are amplified by others, and we become closed or oblivious to any differing philosophy presented. It can sometimes show up in religious arguments too. Polarization and dissonance result. The Bellwether Effect, and the forerunners who promote their processes, prescribe a paradigm. Many management and leadership theories and philosophies fall into the same level of "stuckness" and are the principal cause of the grief experienced by so many who labor today in uninspiring organizations that are still using the eight obsolete business practices discussed in this book. We continue to support these obsolete practices because they are the paradigm we have learned and with which we feel comfortable.

Our habits thus become ingrained, and our ability to be original or enquiring dies. As the pioneering U.S. environmentalist Donella Meadows stated, "Your paradigm is so intrinsic to your mental process that you are hardly aware of its existence, until you try to communicate with someone with a different paradigm." Many theorists believe that the essentials of personality formation are completed by the age of seven,[69] and if this is so, our personal paradigms may be fixed much earlier in our lives than we are prepared to accept. When we

---

69 "Personality Set for Life By 1st Grade, Study Suggests," *Live Science*: https://
    www.livescience.com/8432-personality-set-life-1st-grade-study-suggests.html

act like seven-year-olds, this may be the level of personal development at which some of us have maxed out!

We can get out of this "box" by replacing our natural desire to say, "I don't agree with you!" with "What can I learn from you and your differing perspective?" In fact, the key to change is always about asking questions instead of pressing your point of view ever more loudly onto others—listening more than speaking, being open rather than closed, being a *learner* more than a *knower*.

There are two kinds of people in the world—knowers and learners. Knowers have made up their minds about what they know, have set their beliefs and world views, are certain that they are "right," prefer to live inside their paradigm, and enjoy pressing their beliefs onto everyone else.

Learners understand that everything is changing and information is fluid, have the humility to understand that others also have insights and wisdom, and they are always asking questions (rather than providing answers) and remain open to fresh ideas and perspectives.

Knowers tend to harden their beliefs and polarize people because they are convinced that they (and some-times, they alone!) hold the keys to wisdom.

Are you a knower, skeptical and sometimes cynical and so sure of your beliefs that you are closed to any others?

Or are you a learner who is curious, searching, refreshing your ideas, and updating your knowledge—a contemporary thinker?

Think about the different perspectives expressed in this book. Which chapter created the most discomfort for you because it described a different perspective (paradigm) from your own? Reread that chapter and see what you can learn, what inspires you, how you can adapt some of the ideas without compromising your own values, and how you can grow. Approach that chapter with fresh eyes—as a learner rather than a knower. How can you be more open, and less closed? *Your* world, and therefore *the* world, will be better for it.

2. THE EGO

The ego is an interesting paradox. On the one hand, it receives more than its fair share of criticism for being too domineering, self-serving, narcissistic, aggressive, and more. On the other hand, without our egos we would be nothing—we would not accomplish great things, make a difference in the world, act in plays, excel in sports, write memoirs, have successful careers, or lead others. Like the shadow and the light, we need the ego—*as long as it serves others and we do not serve it.*

As I mentioned earlier, paradigms can be a trap because being stuck in a particular paradigm suffocates change. When we are locked into the sureness of our paradigm, we invest significant ego energy in defending the certainty that we are right. From within our boxes (or paradigms)—for example, the "leader-as-warrior" paradigm—we feel especially threatened by concepts like love, oneness, or the soul. This is because leaders locked in a leader-as-warrior paradigm regard themselves as the inheritors of Darwinian notions of organizational evolutionary survival—since we are on top of the corporate food chain, this argument goes, then who is anyone else (who, by inference, are lesser beings) to challenge this? A certain intellectual smugness results, and like-minded thinkers close ranks to support each other. This creates what is commonly referred to as the "echo chamber," a phenomenon where we listen only to those who repeat versions of our own beliefs and values. Both mainstream media and social media strongly influence and reinforce such an approach. This is a deliberately created paradigm—just three technology corporations hold more power today than religion (another paradigm) or governments, and thus a deliberately created echo chamber is the widespread result. We even hire employees who share the same beliefs so that we can embed our existing routines and processes even more deeply. So, for example, to question the wisdom of the leader-as-warrior paradigm is to risk seeming "odd" or out of step with traditional thinking, and to do so carries political risks that threaten the ego. In other words, introducing concepts outside of the norm of current corporate culture (a paradigm) is to risk a defeat to the ego. As Carl Jung said, "The experience of the self is always a defeat for the ego." The main impediment to change, therefore, is the lack of the necessary courage to accept a temporary bruising of the ego.

A case study in the courage required to leave an old paradigm and brave the inevitable defeat of the ego can be found in the example of Satya Nadella, the CEO of Microsoft, America's 28th-largest company. The old (ego-centered) paradigm at Microsoft was, "A PC on every desk and in every home, running Microsoft software." The new (other-centered) paradigm is, "To empower every person and every organization on the planet to achieve more." When you change the paradigm, you change everything—as Microsoft did when it adopted a new dream. The defeat of the ego is both temporary and worthwhile. In the first three and a half years following Nadella's appointment as CEO, he resurrected a moribund Microsoft and generated more than $250 billion in additional market value—more than Uber and Airbnb, Netflix and Spotify, or Snapchat and WeWork.[70]

What is your current paradigm—personally and organizationally? What would you like it to be? Do you think there is no room for love in the workplace? Then re-read Chapter 2 about moving from fear to love and, with an open mind, see what nuggets you can pull from

---

70 "Satya Nadella Rewrites Microsoft's Code," Harry McCracken, *Fast Company:* https://www.fastcompany.com/40457458/satya-nadella-rewrites-microsofts-code

it. What do you need to change in order to manifest a new and inspiring reality? Is there a chapter in this book that challenged your paradigm the most? What can you learn from that? If you have the necessary courage, then once again, y*our* world, and therefore *the* world, will change. As Joel Barker put it, "Usually the first problems you solve with the new paradigm are the ones that were unsolvable with the old paradigm."

3. THE COPYFROG EFFECT

How often have you sat in a meeting and listened to someone proposing an idea that you considered fatuous, while you remained silent?

When we do this, we remain part of the silent, and therefore invisible, majority, knowing deep inside that we are inauthentic, living a lie, and afraid to step out and speak our truth. When we do this, we are listening to the social self, not the essential self.

An old, but false, urban legend helps to illustrate what can happen to us if we fail to be courageous by challenging the status quo, or the perceived attitudes and opinions of others. According to the legend, if you drop a frog into a pot of hot water, it will quickly jump out, but if you drop the frog into a pot of cold water and gradually raise the temperature, the frog will not react to the rising heat and will eventually cook to death.[71] You might expect that the frog would say, "Hey! Something is wrong here, let's check this out—in fact, let's check out of this pot!" But the frog is either too embarrassed to say anything or doesn't notice the changing environment until it's too late. Like the frog, we are often too busy and too distracted to analyze situations objectively and thoroughly, or to pay attention to the changing ideas and conditions around us with open minds. Our failure to do so results, at best, in missed opportunities, and at worst, in our demise. Thus we remain on the trailing edge rather than the leading edge of innovation, effectiveness, performance, and relationships.

Another metaphorical animal is the copycat: someone who copies the words or behavior of another. Copycat organizations follow the Bellwether forerunners. Join these two critters together and we have a *copyfrog*— someone who is afraid to speak up for fear of ridicule or feeling alone, or appearing not to be a team player, even though many others on the team may feel the same way and are just as afraid to speak out as we are. The others who disagree don't say anything, and neither do we, so the result is that we copy the perceived (but not the real) beliefs of each other—we copy others who are copying us! The c*opyfrog effect* causes us to perpetuate, and inadvertently endorse, the existing paradigm because,

---

71 This is a metaphor used to illustrate a point—it has been proven to be biologically incorrect—see: https://en.wikipedia.org/wiki/Boiling_frog

though it is being questioned silently by many, silence makes it outwardly appear as though we were the only ones doing so—what Leslie Perlow has called the "vicious spiral of silence."[72] Irving Janis described this pattern in his book, *Groupthink,* a classic of social psychology based on the idea that people in groups tend to think differently and, by implication, less effectively than they would have thought as individuals on the same issue at the same time.[73]

With this misunderstanding, a paradox occurs: we march in lockstep, supporting an obsolete or unpopular paradigm with which we don't agree. A decision is made, we disagree with it, but we don't say anything, and as a result, we experience dissonance. This is how unpopular wars begin, poor decisions get made, and superior strategy is degraded. It's the source of broken relationships and dysfunctional teams. It is the reason why some of the obsolete business practices described in this book continue, despite their ineffectiveness and unpopularity and the fact that they cause widespread dissonance. And because authentic conversations are difficult in these conditions, it is a key reason why change is resisted. American print and television journalist Germany Kent points out that "To say nothing is saying

72 *When You Say Yes but Mean No: How Silencing Conflict Wrecks Relationships and Companies...and What You Can Do About It,* Leslie Perlow, Crown Business, 2003; ISBN-13: 978-1400046003

73 *Groupthink: Psychological Studies of Policy Decisions and Fiascoes,* 2nd edition, Irving L. Janis, 1982 ISBN-13: 978-0395317044

something. You must denounce things you are against or one might believe that you support things you really do not."

Consider the ideas presented in this book—do some of the ideas, policies, proposals, recommendations, or decisions run against your grain? If so, muster your courage—ensure that your voice is heard (in an inspiring way) and seek to understand and improve on what you have learned. (Even write to me!) This will help you to avoid becoming a copyfrog. If you are in a meeting where a proposal is put forward with which you disagree, will you speak out—in an inspiring way—to learn more so that you can understand better, or challenge the proposal so that it becomes modified, stronger, and improved, so that you can passionately embrace it?

4. CONFORMITY: FEAR OF BEING OUT-OF-SYNC WITH SOCIETY'S VALUES OR NORMS

We all claim that to love one another and tell the truth is the right way to live our lives, and many of us claim that this is how we actually *do* live our lives. All of the great religions and faith-based philosophies direct us to do so, and the majority of us claim to follow a religion, a spiritual path, or an ancient wisdom and its attendant tenets.

But these spiritual values often do not have a voice in "the real world" of our political, social, and economic practices. While our spiritual values encourage us to be generous, truthful, loving, compassionate, and caring, our quest for the "American Dream" or "personal success," or simply "more" (our urge to meet the needs of the social self) may be guided instead by the pursuit of wealth, reputation, or power—or all three. It may be completely logical that we should love all human beings—in fact, it would be illogical to argue against this—yet we may feel that society's values suggest that "love" in the workplace is flakey, too out there, or risky, and therefore our egos could be bruised—a misinformed social self that imposes its will upon us. To avoid a defeat of our ego, we bend to the norms of society, and so logic is trumped by ego—a victory for the social self. Frequently, we can find our personal values in opposition to the values of society. While we profess to believe that we should be kind to our competitors and generous to our political opponents, the very terms "competitor" and "opponent" make these empty aspirations. Thus we are condemned to living inauthentic lives—at home and at work. The ego wants us to appear strong and invincible instead of vulnerable, humble, and transparent. We know exactly what we should do; we even know what we really *want* to do, but we have lost our voice and our courage to do so. We are hostage to our ego. In the debate between the essential self and the social self, the social self too often wins.

Before we can embrace change, therefore, we must embrace courage, the first of the CASTLE® Principles. It takes courage to swim against the current. It takes courage to say, "I don't know," "I need your help," "I was wrong," "Your idea is better than mine." It takes courage to be mindful of (but not controlled by) what others will think or say or how they will judge us. It takes courage to say, "I have always done it this way, but perhaps there is a better way." In other words, it takes courage to be open-minded, to welcome new or different ideas and to set aside ego and defensiveness— to give the essential self more airtime. It takes courage to step from the known to the unknown.

Courage requires us to:

- *Make a personal commitment to our own higher principles*
- *Be aware of and accept the risks involved in living by those principles*
- *Be willing to accept the consequences of those risks*

Rollo May said, "The opposite of courage in our society is not cowardice, it's conformity"—the Bellwether Effect.

To sum up, then, to embrace change, we need to:

1. be conscious of, and willingly listen to, the **paradigms** of others besides our own;

2. keep our **egos** in check by avoiding hubris— our paradigm may not necessarily be *the only* paradigm;

3. not be "**copyfrogs**" by silencing our voices and mimicking the opinions or behaviors of others;

4. not be tempted to **conform** because we are intimidated by social pressures and *society's opposing values* when they do not align with our own.

If we do these four things, we will improve our chances of willingly embracing change. Or we can choose to stay in a (currently) comfortable place. As Charles Darwin famously said, "It is not the strongest of the species that survive, nor the most intelligent, but the one most responsive to change."

The Bellwether Effect can sometimes feel like moss growing on a stone—slowly layering itself into the organization, until someone asks, "Why are we doing this? How did this get started? What is the current benefit and value of this? Is there a better way?" This is when creative minds challenge the status quo and welcome change, seeking to reinvent business processes, bending them to the needs of people, instead of the other way around. This is when ineffective and long-endured business processes are replaced by new ways that serve and inspire people. As veteran MIT researcher Donald Schon points out, "The new idea either finds a champion or it dies. No ordinary involvement with a new idea provides the energy required to cope with the indifference and resistance that change provokes."

How ready are you to embrace change? Which of the core ideas in this book are you open to considering and implementing? What would prevent you? Your social self? What does your essential self *really* want to do? How will you use the four steps above to help you and your organization make a breakthrough and move beyond the Bellwether Effect?

The ideas in this book represent significant change and a departure from existing paradigms. As the reader, you have been invited to explore, investigate, validate, and research these ideas to test their applicability. Implementing these ideas will require a change in organizational culture and a paradigm shift. Neither of these is easy because, for the reasons outlined above, most of us do not want to change. There will also be resistance and criticism. But when we stop focusing on what we may have to give up and, instead, focus on what we will gain, we will create the kind of organizations for whom people want to work, and with whom customers and vendors want to do business, and a world where we enjoy the support that comes from inspiring relationships with every stakeholder. We can leave the dysfunctional business processes unchanged, or we can update and replace them and therefore move the needle on every important high-performance metric. The choice is yours, and restoring our passion for corporate life depends on it.

ACKNOWLEDGMENTS

I am indebted to my friends, clients, and colleagues who have supported my work over many years, helped me to "noodle" my theories and philosophies, encouraged me when I would disappear down a rabbit hole, challenged, and therefore strengthened, nascent thoughts and helped me to burnish them and bring them into fully formed concepts.

Thank you to readers of early drafts of my manuscript who offered advice, criticism, creativity, support and insights: Barb Siray, Bill Jensen, Bob Dryburgh, Bruce Broussard, Catherine Wood, Cesar Cernuda, Claude Cloutier, Constance Scrafield, Dan Kuyper, Dave Blair, Dave Mowat, Dave Nyburg, Deanna Hatmaker, Deanna Stull, Debra Canales, Debbie McGrath, Ellie Filler, Erika Caspersen, Francisco Sorrentino, Frank Costantini, Gina Mazza, Jack Cox, Jehangir Daruwala, Jim Wilson, Joe Reagan, John Pryor, Justin Holland, Ken Bloom, Marc Hanlan, Michael Humphrey, Mike McCallister, Mike McCuaig, Paul Kusserow, Penelope Fridman, Raja Rajamannar, Randy Knipping, Roger Steinkruger, Scott Ginnetti, Steve Farrell, Steve Hultquist, Susan Grindle, Sylvia Vogt, Tom Noland, and Wahn Yoon.

Thanks to the brilliant team of many years and many books: Tricia Field of the Secretan Center Inc.; Simone Gabbay, my editor; Heidy Lawrance and her design team at WeMakeBooks; Fred Cheetham and the printers at Friesens Corporation; Jack Werner of Cattails Multimedia; Allan Thornton of Sixth Realm Interactive Media; and Eva Henry of Eva Henry Art.

INDEX

ABOUT THE SECRETAN CENTER INC.

The Secretan Center Inc. is an award-winning global advisory firm specializing in corporate and personal transformation, working with, coaching, and inspiring leaders, and their teams, to create inspiring organizations that change the world.

For Companies and Governmental, Non-Profit, and Academic Organizations

If you would like to discuss the possibility of introducing Higher Ground Leadership® to your organization, please contact the Secretan Center Inc. at info@secretan.com

For Individuals

We offer training and certification programs for individuals seeking personal growth and development in both leadership and coaching. If you would like to learn more about our leadership or coach training, credentialing, and certification programs, please visit http://www.secretan.com/training/credentialing/

Coaching

If you would like to invite Lance Secretan to be your coach, or if you would like one of our other certified coaches to support you, please send us an email to info@secretan.com or contact us at: www.secretan.com/contact-us/

Keynotes

Lance Secretan is ranked among the top 10 leadership speakers in the world. If you would like him to deliver a keynote presentation to your conference, please visit: http://www.secretan.com/book-lance/

ABOUT THE AUTHOR

Dr. Lance Secretan is a pioneering philosopher whose bestselling books, inspirational talks, and life-changing retreats have touched the hearts and minds of hundreds of thousands of people worldwide. He is the author of 21 books about leadership, inspiration, corporate culture, and entrepreneurship, as well as an award-winning memoir, *A Love Story*. Lance is a riveting speaker and is acknowledged globally as one of our most insightful and original leadership teachers. He is the former CEO of a *Fortune* 100  company, university professor, award-winning columnist, poet, author, and outdoor athlete. He coaches and advises leaders globally (he is ranked among both the Top 30 Most Influential Executive Coaches and the Top 30 Most Influential Leadership Experts in the world) and guides leadership teams who wish to transform their culture into the most inspirational in their industries.

Individuals, entire organizations, cities, and states have experienced remarkable transformations through his unique wisdom and approach to mentoring and coaching. He has helped six companies to be named to *Fortune's Best Companies to Work For in America* list; eight other companies on this list are also his clients. In addition, thirty Secretan Center clients are on *Fortune's Most Admired Companies* list. Speakers in America ranks Lance Secretan among the Top Five Leadership speakers, and his firm, the Secretan Center Inc., is ranked #1 in the world as an International Leadership Consulting firm by Leadership Excellence.

Dr. Secretan is the recipient of many other awards, including the International Caring Award, whose previous winners include Pope Francis, the Dalai Lama, President Jimmy Carter, and Dr. Desmond Tutu. He is the current Chair of the Pay It Forward Foundation and former Chair of the Advisory Board of the Special Olympics World Winter Games. He is an expert skier, kayaker, and mountain biker, and he divides his time between Ontario, Canada and the Colorado Rockies.